PRIMARY PARTNERS

Quick-and-Easy Ways to Achievement Days

for Girls Ages 8-11

24 Goal Activities with:
Invitations
Icebreaker Activities
Goal Activities
Success Snacks

Fun Theme Parties!
— Zap Boredom with Zippy Achievement Days
— Buttons and Bows Daddy Daughter Date
— Dress and Dazzle! Mom and Me Fashion Show

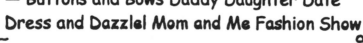

Quarterly Motivation and Award Activities:
— Fishing for Success!
— Clowning Around Carnival
— Hats Off to You!
— You're the Star!

Printed in the United States of America
First Printing: September 2001

Primary Partners: Quick-and-Easy Achievement Days - Ages 8-11

Covenant Communications, Inc.
American Fork, Utah

ISBN 1-57734-956-3

INTRODUCTION
Quick-and-Easy Ways to Achievement Days
Achievement Days is to help girls ages 8-11 achieve goals in 12 areas:

> Arts and Crafts   Education and Scholarship   Family History   Family Skills
> Health and Personal Grooming   Hospitality   Outdoor Fun and Skills
> Personal Preparedness   Safety and Emergency Preparedness
> Service and Citizenship   Spirituality   Sports and Physical Fitness

With this volume of *Primary Partners* Quick-and-Easy Ways to Achievement Days, every detail is worked out for you, allowing you to concentrate on the different personalities and needs of each girl. You'll find 24 theme activities representing the 12 goal areas, and with each theme you will find an invitation, icebreaker activity, goal activity, and a "success snack."

You will also find a Zip Over to Achievement Days motivational party to introduce Achievement Days, a Buttons and Bows Daddy Daughter Date, a Mom and Me Fashion Show, and four Quarterly Motivation and Award Activities: Fishing for Success, Clowning Around Carnival, Hats off to You! and You're a Star! Each party/activity is complete with invitation, games and activities, treats, and matching theme certificates for quarterly activities.

10 Ways to Quick-and-Easy Achievement Days:

#1—GOAL CARDS explain each goal step-by-step. Give these out during the activity to review the goal! The goal card and supplies can also be given to individual girls later, who can work on each goal on their own or enlist the help of a parent or Achievement Days friend.

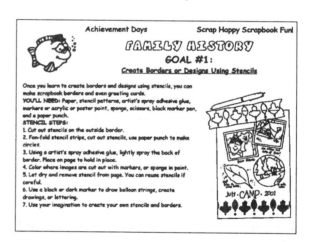

#2—PLAN ACTIVITIES ahead using the Zip on Over to Achievement Days schedule (page @).

#3—COPY OR PRINT invitations, goal motivation cards (on invitation page), and patterns for each activity. All of the activities and patterns from this book can be printed in color or black and white, using the *Primary Partners: Quick-and-Easy Ways to Achievement Days* CD-ROM (shown left).

#4—MAKE INVITATION and deliver a week ahead of time or give out at Achievement Day two weeks earlier to increase attendance and participation.

#5—REMIND GIRLS of activities. Assign different girls each month to be the secretary to call and remind others about the activity and what to bring. The "secretary" might even deliver the invitations personally.

#6—GATHER SUPPLIES.

#7—REVIEW ICEBREAKER ACTIVITIES.

#8—MAKE AHEAD a sample of the finished goal project.

#9—MAKE SUCCESS SNACKS ahead or during the activity.

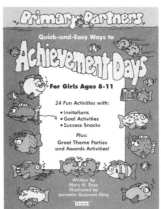

#10—ENJOY OTHER ACHIEVEMENT DAYS TOOLS:
Tool #1: *Primary Partners Achievement Days* book and CD-ROM by Mary Ross and Jennette Guymon-King with 24 more goal activities, invitations, parties, and more.

Tool #2: *Primary Partners: Clip-Art on CD-ROM,* with the 12 Achievement Day balloon symbols (to use instead of the fish symbols used in this book).

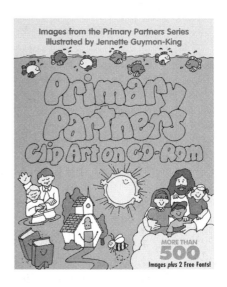

You will find 36 borders and hundreds of images and headlines to use for various Achievement Days projects (scrapbooks, award buttons, etc.).

• CD-ROM includes 500 images you can print in color or black and white, plus two free fonts: Primary Poster and Primary Print.

TABLE OF CONTENTS

OUTDOOR FUN & SKILLS

PERSONAL PREPAREDNESS

SAFETY & EMERGENCY PREPAREDNESS

SERVICE & CITIZENSHIP

SPIRITUALITY

SPORTS & PHYSICAL FITNESS

PARTIES AND RECOGNITION

GOAL MOTIVATION PARTY
Zap Boredom with Zippy Achievement Days!

OBJECTIVE: Use at the beginning or anytime during the year to help girls learn Achievement Days goals and create an organizer.

YOU'LL NEED: Copies of patterns (pages 3-7): invitation, cookie recipe, and zipper notebook calendar and labels for each girl, one set of Achievement Days clue cards. Obtain a school folder with two pockets inside, and a "My Achievement Days" goal booklet for each girl. Purchase a bag of Smarties candies or other motivational treat, and Zippy "Z" Cookie ingredients.

Zip on over for an
Achievement Days Party !

Date: _____
Time: _____
Place: _____

See you there!

ZIPPY INVITATION: Color and cut out invitations, fill in details and deliver 1-2 week before activity.

ACTIVITIES:

• PLAY THE ZIPPY ACHIEVEMENT DAYS GOAL REVIEW GAME:
Color and cut out one set clue cards.

TO PLAY:

1. Lay the clue cards in front of girls with goals face down.
2. Divide girls into two teams to sit across from each other.
3. Provide for girls a list of the 12 Achievement Days goal areas found on the notebook calendar labels (shown right).
4. Have teams take turns drawing a clue card from the pile and reading one clue at a time to their team, giving them 30 seconds to guess. If they can't guess, the other team has a chance to reveal the Achievement Days goal area that matches the clues. Repeat clues if needed.
5. If no one guesses, reveal the goal area.
6. Keep going until all goals have been guessed or revealed.

7. Give one point for each goal area guessed, adding up points to determine winners.
8. Award the winning team with two Smarties candy and the losing team with one Smarties.

• **MAKE SUCCESS SNACK**: <u>Zippy "Z" Achievement Days Cookies</u>. Make the dough ahead. Copy recipe for girls to take home. Recipe makes 32 cookies. With the "Z"-shaped cookies girls can be reminded of their zippy Achievement Days goals. They can do this by topping each cookie with 12 candies representing the 12 goal areas. As they create and eat their cookies, discuss how they can add more zip to their life by achieving goals. While cookies are baking, girls can work on their Zippy Notebook.

• **MAKE ZIPPY NOTEBOOK:**

<u>To Make Notebook</u>.

1. Give each girl a school folder with two inside pockets and notebook calendar and labels (pages 5-6) to decorate her notebook.

2. Color and cut out notebook labels.

3. Glue the calendar on the cover and labels on the inside left and right pockets (to write goals).

4. Show girls how they can slip their goal handouts and activities in the pockets.

5. Plan the year's calendar in advance so girls can record on their calendar upcoming Achievement Days activities.

6. Girls can check boxes on the inside checklist as they achieve their goals.

2

Zip on over for an
Achievement Days Party !

Date: _____
Time: _____
Place: _____
_____
See you there!

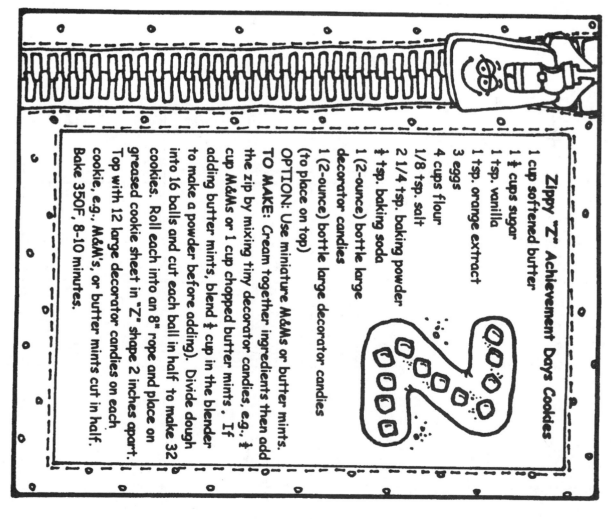

Zippy "Z" Achievement Days Cookies

1 cup softened butter
1 ½ cups sugar
1 tsp. vanilla
1 tsp. orange extract
3 eggs
4 cups flour
1/8 tsp. salt
2 1/4 tsp. baking powder
½ tsp. baking soda
1 (2-ounce) bottle large decorator candies
1 (2-ounce) bottle large decorator candies

OPTION: Use miniature M&Ms or butter mints.
(to place on top)

TO MAKE: Cream together ingredients then add the zip by mixing tiny decorator candies, e.g., ½ cup M&Ms or 1 cup chopped butter mints. If adding butter mints, blend ½ cup in the blender to make a powder before adding). Divide dough into 16 balls and cut each ball in half to make 32 cookies. Roll each into an 8" rope and place on greased cookie sheet in "Z" shape 2 inches apart. Top with 12 large decorator candies on each cookie, e.g., M&M's, or butter mints cut in half. Bake 350F, 8-10 minutes.

Family History

Clues:
1. Learn about kin
2. Pen your memories
3. Search records
4. Make a family tree

Hospitality

Clues:
1. Make a friend
2. Mind your manners
3. Have games on hand
4. Remember names

Education & Scholarship

Clues:
1. Increase your I.Q.
2. Book look
3. Make the grade
4. Listen and learn

Health & Personal Grooming

Clues:
1. Eat healthful foods
2. Take vitamins
3. Be clean and orderly
4. Wear modest clothes

Arts & Crafts

Clues:
1. Being creative
2. Being dramatic
3. Crooning a tune
4. Writing rhymes

Family Skills

Clues:
1. Change a diaper
2. Bake a cake
3. Mend a sock
4. Squeaky clean

Safety & Emergency Preparedness

Clues:
1. Know first-aid
2. Learn survival skills
3. Know self-defense
4. Protect children

Personal Preparedness

Clues:
1. Use an organizer
2. Live on a budget
3. Stock up on storage
4. Learn a home career

Outdoor Fun & Skills

Clues:
1. Barbecue
2. Read a compass
3. Take a hike
4. Save a ladybug

Sports & Physical Fitness

Clues:
1. Play fun games
2. Be a good sport
3. Learn fitness
4. Exercise

Spirituality

Clues:
1. Share the gospel
2. Read the *New Era*
3. Learn a scripture
4. Memorize the Articles of Faith

Service & Citizenship

Clues:
1. Visit the elderly
2. Help the sick
3. Pitch in and help
4. Learn laws

Zip on over to Achievement Days!

January
Date: _____
Time: _____
Place: _____
_____

May
Date: _____
Time: _____
Place: _____
_____

September
Date: _____
Time: _____
Place: _____
_____

February
Date: _____
Time: _____
Place: _____
_____

June
Date: _____
Time: _____
Place: _____
_____

October
Date: _____
Time: _____
Place: _____
_____

March
Date: _____
Time: _____
Place: _____
_____

July
Date: _____
Time: _____
Place: _____
_____

November
Date: _____
Time: _____
Place: _____
_____

April
Date: _____
Time: _____
Place: _____

August
Date: _____
Time: _____
Place: _____

December
Date: _____
Time: _____
Place: _____

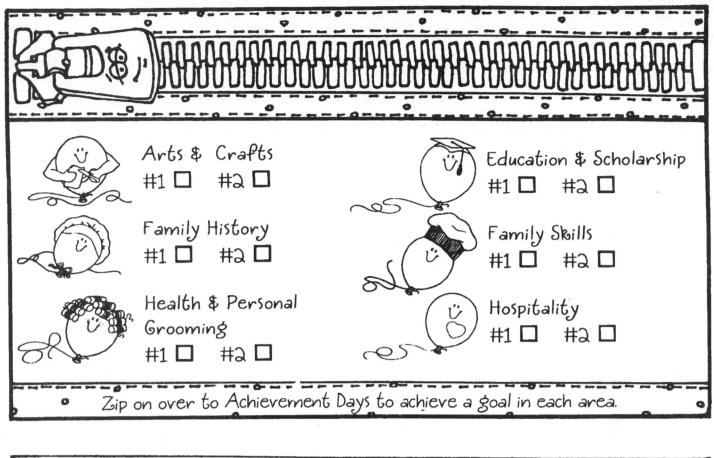

Arts & Crafts
#1 ☐ #2 ☐

Family History
#1 ☐ #2 ☐

Health & Personal
Grooming
#1 ☐ #2 ☐

Education & Scholarship
#1 ☐ #2 ☐

Family Skills
#1 ☐ #2 ☐

Hospitality
#1 ☐ #2 ☐

Zip on over to Achievement Days to achieve a goal in each area.

Outdoor Fun & Skills
#1 ☐ #2 ☐

Safety & Emergency
Preparedness
#1 ☐ #2 ☐

Spirituality
#1 ☐ #2 ☐

Personal Preparedness
#1 ☐ #2 ☐

Service & Citizenship
#1 ☐ #2 ☐

Sports & Physical Fitness
#1 ☐ #2 ☐

Once your goal has been completed, place a check in the appropriate box.

ARTS & CRAFTS

Theme #1: Drawing Fun!

Invitation: Copy-and-create invitation (page 9) to give to girls a week before activity, writing the items you need them to bring, e.g., art supplies and old magazines.

Icebreaker Activity - Silly Draw:

DO AHEAD: Copy the Silly Draw cards (page 10) for each girl and give them a pencil, or use blank cards.

ACTIVITY: Ask girls to draw what you are describing in one minute. Use drawing cues (below). After each drawing have girls show what they drew. It's so fun to see what they all came up with. Have girls help you make up phrases if you wish to continue.

SILLY DRAWING CUES: Use the same letters in the sentence or rhyming words to make it even more fun. Alphabet Silly Draw: (1) Ape ate apple while air-borne (2) Baby in a basket with bib and bottle (3) Cat climbed child's carriage (4) Dog drank dinner dunking doughnuts (5) Elephant's ear was elevated (6) Funny fabulous friend (7) Grumpy goat in a gown Rhyming Silly Draw: (1) The fat cat ate the flat rat. (2) The big goose chased the caboose. (3) The giant egg rolled down the farmer's leg. (4) The snackers ate crackers.

Goal #1 Activity -
Create an All About Me! Collage:

YOU'LL NEED: Copy of goal card (page 9) and the #1-10 and All About Me! sign (page 11), and a large colored poster for each girl, art supplies, and magazines to cut up (requested on the invitation). **ACTIVITY:** Create an All About Me! Collage. See goal card (page 9) for details.

Success Snack — Painted Canvas
Cookies: (1) Have sugar cookie dough ready to
paint with cookie paints (2 tablespoons canned milk with a few drops of food coloring). (2) Have girls cut out a desired shape with a butter knife and paint it with cookie paints. Before they eat they can tell about their painted cookie canvas.

Please come to a
fun and silly activity!

Date: _____
Time: _____
Place: _____

Please bRing: _____

See you theRe!

Achievement Days   ＡＲＴＳ ＆ ＣＲＡＦＴＳ   **Drawing Fun!**

GOAL #1:   <u>Create an All About Me! poster painting or collage</u>.

Design a poster that tells about you. Use the attached glue-on stickers to create a poster story about you.

1. Use your art supplies, e.g., poster paper, construction paper,

markers, acrylic and water paints, pictures from magazines and pictures of you and your family.

If you don't want to use real photos, make photocopies of them.

2. Tell about your life. Start out by making a timeline on a piece of paper and writing main

events you want to draw or specific things about yourself you want to put on the poster (your favorite color, music, things to do, movies, hobbies, trips or family outings, your friends, family, ancestors, school, etc.).

3. Place the words All About Me! at the top and put your autograph (name) below as the artist.

4. Girls can make their poster using a numbered 1-10 sequence to tell 10 things about themselves, or they can mix up the images, creating a collage.

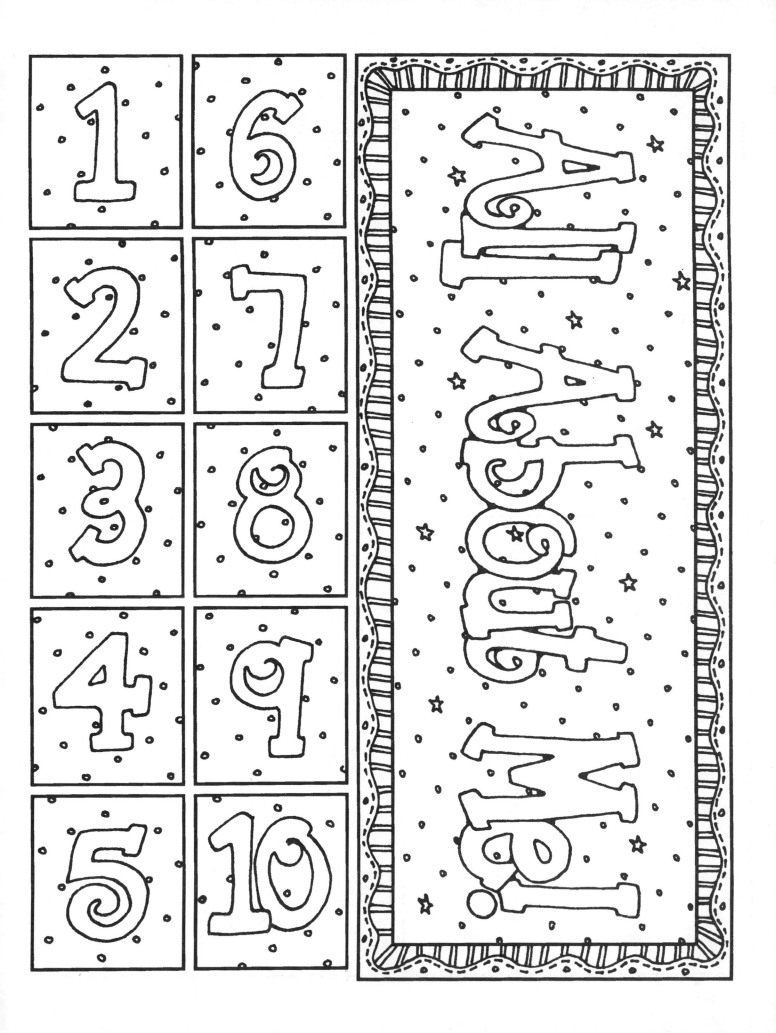

ARTS & CRAFTS
Theme #2: I'm "Sew" Happy!

Invitation: Copy-and-create invitation (page 13) to give to girls a week before activity. Write on the invitation the items you want them to bring* (see below).

Icebreaker Activity – I'm "Sew" Happy! Demo:

YOU'LL NEED: Copy of the scripture cover instructions (pages 14-17), a blue hardback Book of Mormon, and supplies listed below. Make ahead one scripture cover to show.

ACTIVITY: Show a scripture cover already made. Show girls how they can take it out, put it in the cover, and how they can snap or Velcro it closed. **DEMO** how one is made step-by-step as you have girls make theirs (detailed below and on the scripture cover instruction pages).

Goal #2 Activity: Sew a Scripture Cover:

OBJECTIVE: Girls can make a travel Book of Mormon cover that they can take to camp, school, or on a trip. They would enclose in the cover a less expensive copy of the Book of Mormon and keep their more expensive book safe at home. Plus, they could give this copy away if they wanted.

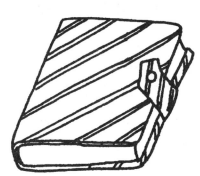

YOU'LL NEED: Copy of goal card and scripture cover instructions (pages 14-17) for each girl and supplies*, sewing machine or needle and thread, plus fabric*.

*Write on the invitation items you want girls to bring—a standard blue hardback Book of Mormon and a 9" x 23" quilted fabric scrap.

ACTIVITY: Create a fabric scripture cover detailed on instructions. Also see goal card (page 13).

Success Snack -Sewing Sweets:

Idea #1: <u>Sewing Needle Cookies</u>. Cut out large needle shapes from sugar cookie dough, punching a hole with a tiny bottle lid. Bake and thread licorice string through the hole. Make extras to take home.

Idea #2: <u>Pincushion cupcakes</u>. Frost cupcakes and place three or four colored toothpicks on top with small gumdrops cut in half or jelly beans stuck on top (to look like pins).

Idea #3: <u>Button Cookies</u>. Frost cookies on top with a cake decorator tube, making a circle around the edge of a round cookie and four dots in the center (to look like button holes). Frost an X-shape joining the four dots (to look like thread).

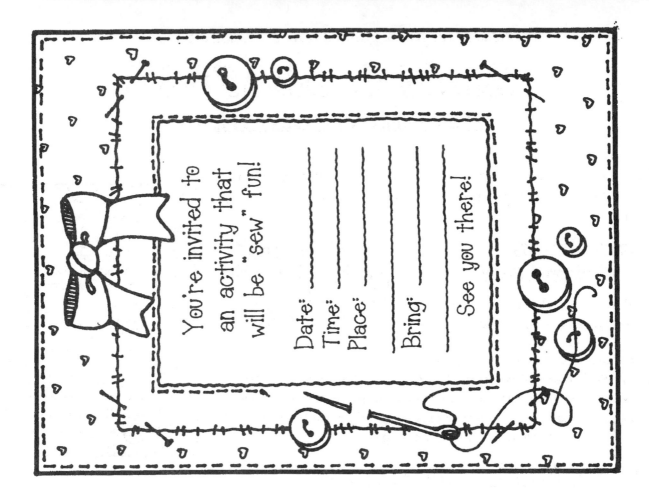

You're invited to
an activity that
will be "sew" fun!

Date:
Time:
Place:
Bring:

See you there!

Achievement Days   ARTS & CRAFTS   I'm "Sew" Happy!

GOAL #2: <u>Sew a Scripture Cover</u>

This is "sew" simple, you will want to stitch up a scripture cover for your friends and family.

Make a Book of Mormon scripture cover to enclose a less-expensive copy of the Book of Mormon that you can carry with you to camp, school, or on a trip. Then you can leave your more expensive book safe at home. Plus, you could give this copy away to a friend who would like to read it. Then, make another.

YOU'LL NEED: A standard Book of Mormon and a 9" x 23" quilted fabric scrap, felt, or vinyl, and a snap or Velcro.

TO MAKE: Adjust pattern for larger or smaller books. Girls can hand stitch this or use a machine. Simply follow the instructions on the pattern sheets, make the handle, and sew on Velcro or add a snap to close.

BOOK OF MORMON PROJECT: If you are giving away copies of the Book of Mormon to friends, make a scripture cover in their favorite color. Be sure to add your testimony and picture inside.

Book Cover Sewing Instructions

1. <u>Pattern</u>: Tape together pattern pieces 1a and 1b before placing on fabric for cutting out. Be sure to note which pattern edges must be placed on the fold for cutting.

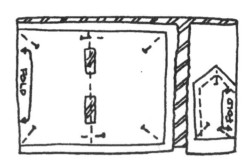

2. <u>Cutting</u>: For a basic book cover, quilted fabric scrap should be at least 9" wide and 23" long. Pin where needed to secure pattern and cut out as shown. Be sure to place fold edges on folded fabric where indicated for both pattern pieces.

3. <u>Sewing</u>: A. To start, fold both ends of the cover over ½ inch and stitch on wrong side. Do not allow stitches to show on the other side.

B. To ensure a proper fit and for ease in sewing, pin the cover wrong side out on the book as shown. Sew top and bottom of both flaps close to the book but not too snugly. Once cover is turned right side out, a little room is needed for the seam or the book covers will not fit into the flaps. Trim the sewn seam a little if edge is too bulky.

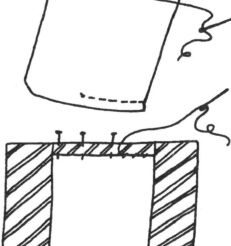

C. Once top and bottom of front and back flaps are sewn, turn the cover right side out. Fold down edges between flaps and pin in place. Stitch edge carefully so stitches do not show through to the other side. Sew down both top and bottom edges.

D. Stitch together edges of the snap closure, leaving the bottom open to turn closure right side out. Trim corners (but not too close to stitching) so that when closure is turned right side out the corners will not bulge. After the closure is turned right side out, press if needed.

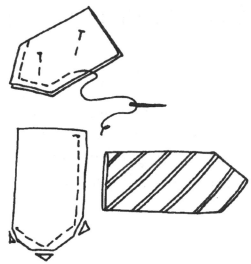

E. Sew snap closure to cover. Sew approximately ¾ inch of closure to inside flap. Be sure to sew to inside flap only and not through to front cover or book will not fit into the flap. Sew closure securely on all three sides and secure closure to the outside edge, hiding the stitching.

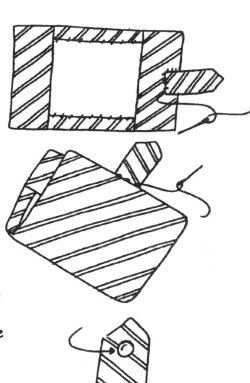

4. Snap: Secure snap according to instructions on the snap package. One side of the snap should be placed on the closure as shown. To place the other side of the snap on the front cover, put book inside cover, then folding closure over to the front, mark the spot with a pencil or chalk where the other side of the snap should be secured. Remove the book from the cover and attach the second half of the snap in the place marked. When attaching the snap to the cover side, be sure to move the flap away from the area so the snap is secured only to the front and not all the way through to the flap.

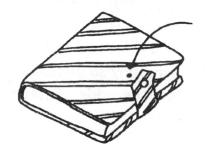

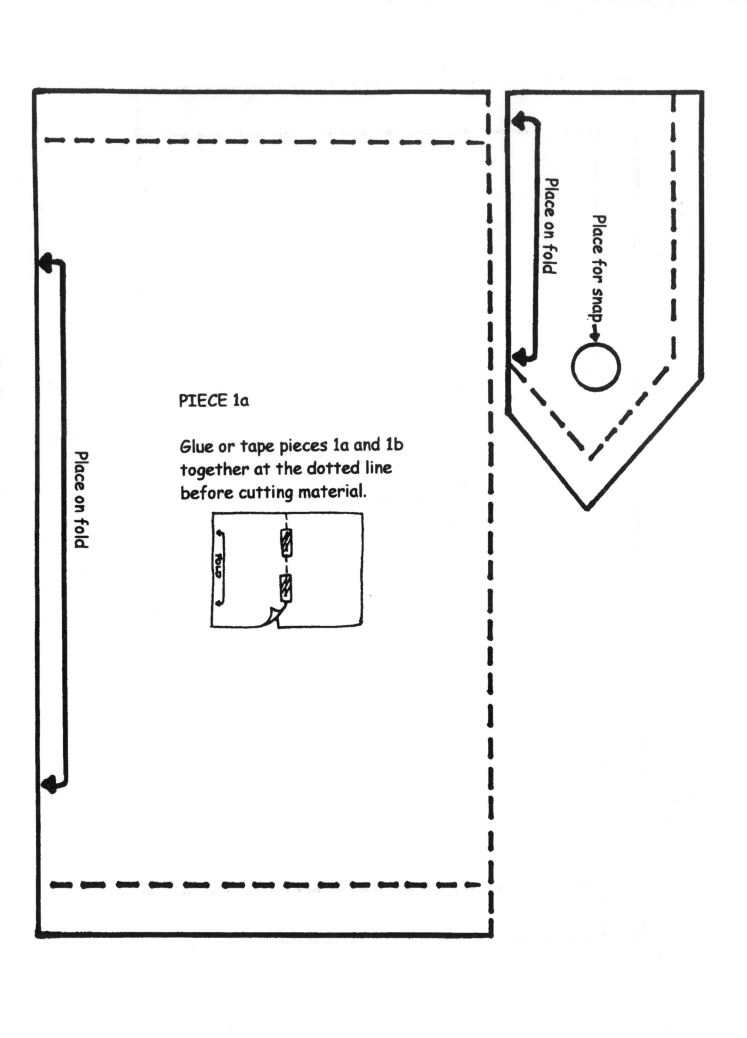

PIECE 1a

Glue or tape pieces 1a and 1b together at the dotted line before cutting material.

Place on fold

Place on fold

Place for snap

Place on fold

PIECE 1b

Glue or tape pieces 1a and 1b
together at the dotted line
before cutting material.

Education & Scholarship

Theme #1: Coloring My Life with Knowledge

Invitation: Copy-and-create invitation (page 19) to give girls a week before activity.

Icebreaker Activity - Color My Life with Knowledge Demonstration:

DO AHEAD FOR ACTIVITY #1: Fill five clear glasses 3/4ths full with water, placing a drop of food coloring in four of the five glasses leaving one glass with clear water. Colors to use: red, yellow, green, and blue.

DO AHEAD FOR ACTIVITY #2: Copy the (rose) colored glasses (page 22) on rose-colored cardstock paper for each girl. Purchase red cellophane (available at craft stores) to insert in glasses. Find a few favorite poems to read.

ACTIVITY #1: Colored Water Demonstration:

1. Show glass with clear water (hiding the rest). Tell girls, "Some people drink freely from the fountain of knowledge while others only gargle. Let's learn how we can drink freely from the fountain of knowledge."

2. Show glass with green water. Say, "Caroline and her brother found a pond filled with green frogs hopping merrily, jumping, and sinking into the mud and water. She was so excited that she went to her encyclopedia and learned that boy frogs call out 'jug-o-rum' and girl frogs don't speak out, and in this way she <u>colored her life with knowledge</u>."

3. Show glass with blue water. Say, "One day Alexa went to the ocean and saw the deep blue water. She took some of the ocean water inside to see if it was really blue, and it didn't have color. She later read that pure water is transparent and colorless. Water that is under the sky turns blue, reflecting from the sky. She also learned that there is a song called 'Land of the Sky-Blue Water,' and in this way she <u>colored her life with knowledge</u>."

4. Show glass with yellow water. Say, "One day Kim saw a large sunflower growing over her backyard fence. She found some garden books and read about how to grow giant sunflowers, <u>coloring her life with knowledge</u>."

5. Show glass with red water. Michelle learned that George Washington had supposedly chopped down a cherry tree on his dad's farm (according to his biography, this is only a myth; it never happened). Still, it made Michelle hungry for cherry pie, so she found a cherry pie recipe and made one, which <u>colored her life with knowledge</u>. As we drink from the fountain of knowledge, we color our life each day.

ACTIVITY #2: Rose-Colored Glasses Reading Time: Cut out the Rose Colored Glasses frames (page 21) and tape a 2" x 6" piece of red cellophane behind frames to create lenses. Tell girls that looking through rose-colored glasses means that you are look on the bright side, anticipating the best from life. Have girls take turns reading a short poem wearing their rose colored glasses.

Goal #1 Activity: Color My Life with Knowledge Search

YOU'LL NEED: Copy of goal card and the four "Color my world with knowledge!" cards, (pages 19-21) for each girl.

ACTIVITY: See goal card (page 18) for activity details.

Success Snack - Treats of a Different Color.
Provide a large selection of foods of different colors but cover them. Ask girls for their favorite color, then pull out a sample of food that is their favorite color. They can then eat that food. Ask what their favorite color is ahead of time.

You're invited to
come and learn how to
Color Your World
with knowledge!

Date: _____

Time: _____

Place: _____

_____
_____

See you there!

Achievement Days

Color My Life with Knowledge

EDUCATION & SCHOLARSHIP

GOAL #1:

by completing the seek-and-tell steps below, using the "Color my world with knowledge!" forms.

Color My Life with Knowledge

SEEK-AND-TELL STEPS:

STEP #1: Using the red, yellow, green, and blue forms, write a question you may have about that color. For example, on the green card you might write: "What does it mean when you find a four-leaf clover?"

STEP #2: Research to learn about your color and subject and write it on the form (e.g., "Some people believe that when you find a four-leaf clover, you will have good luck."

STEP #3: Share what you learned.

Color my world with knowledge!

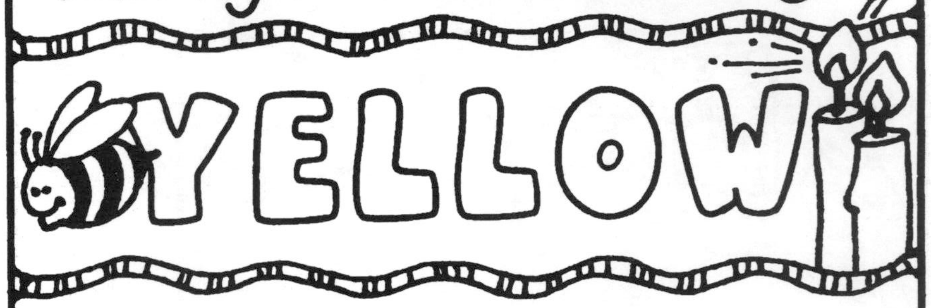

YELLOW

I wondered about...

I learned that...

Color my world with knowledge!

RED

I wondered about...

I learned that...

Color my world with knowledge!

BLUE

I wondered about...

I learned that...

Color my world with knowledge!

GREEN

I wondered about...

I learned that...

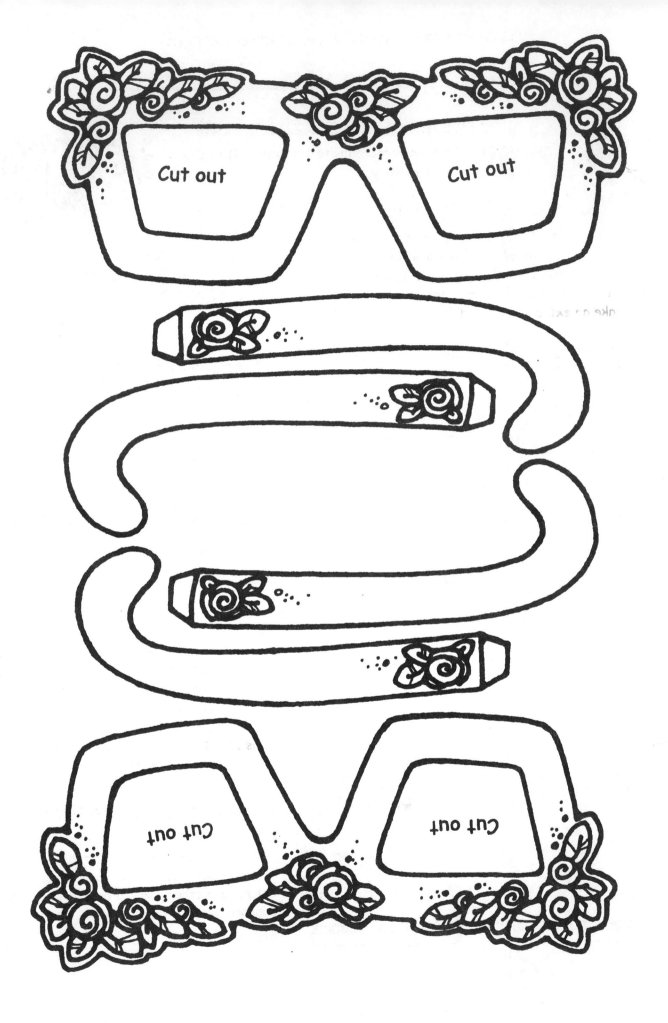

Education & Scholarship

Theme #2: School Is Cool!

Invitation: Copy-and-create invitation (page 24) to give to girls a week before activity.

Icebreaker Activity –
School Is Cool! Match Game:

DO AHEAD: Copy, color, and cut out two sets of match cards (pages 25-26) to make a total of 48 cards, on cardstock paper.

OPTIONAL: Make an extra set of cards for the girls to take home.

REVIEW CARDS: Tell girls that school can be cool if you follow some of these cool rules to have a positive experience with school.

TO PLAY MATCH GAME: Lay a double set of cards face down on the floor or table. Have girls sit around cards to play. If you have a large group or over six girls, divide into teams to play. Take turns turning cards over to make a match. When you make a match, read the completed card. Play until all cards are matched. The team or person with the most matches wins.

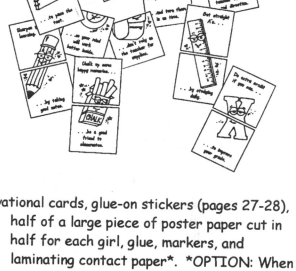

Goal #2 Activity –

Create a Super Study Spot Pad:

YOU'LL NEED: Copy of goal card and Super Study Spot signs, motivational cards, glue-on stickers (pages 27-28), half of a large piece of poster paper cut in half for each girl, glue, markers, and laminating contact paper*. *OPTION: When complete, take poster to a photocopy shop to be laminated.

ACTIVITY: Create a Super Study Spot pad girls can place on their study table or desk. See goal card (page 24) for details.

Success Snack – Healthful

Study Snacks: Share and talk about healthful snacks (brain food) that help keep you alert while you study: apples, carrots, celery, and other raw fruits and vegetables, popcorn, whole grain crackers.

School is cool!
You're invited to a
noteworthy activity!

Date: _____
Time: _____
Place: _____

See you there!

EDUCATION & SCHOLARSHIP

GOAL #2:

Create a Super Study Spot Pad

1. Find a half-size piece of poster paper.
2. Color and cut out the Super Study Spot labels, motivational cards, and glue-on stickers.
3. Glue them on the poster along with pictures to motivate you.
4. Write your name on the poster and goals on the back.
5. Laminate for durability.
6. Now find a desk or quiet place to study and place your Super Study Spot pad there. Then every day study at this spot.
7. Learn more ways to study effectively to make the grades you desire.
8. Remember, completing your assignments on time, listening, studying hard, and doing extra credit work can earn an A.

...so your mind will work better inside.

Do extra credit if you can. . .

...to improve your grade.

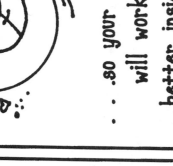

...don't rely on the teacher for supplies.

Review your notes. . .

...to pass the test.

...and turn them in on time.

Chalk up some happy memories. . .

...be a good friend to classmates.

...ask your teacher for help and direction.

Make sure that you always eat right. . . .

...to keep your brain bright!

SUPER

STUDY

SPOT

Healthy food is brain food. I will pick healthy snacks!

School rules!

When I study I stay sharp!

Bless my heart! I'm so smart!

I buzz through my homework because I love to learn!

Concentration is the secret of strength. -R.W. Emerson

FAMILY HISTORY
Theme #1: Scrap Happy Scrapbooking Fun!

Invitation: Copy-and-create invitation (page 30) to give to girls a week before activity, writing the items they need to bring, e.g., photos and scrapbook supplies.

Icebreaker Activity – Learn "Bear"y Fun Ways to Make a Memory Scrapbook:

DO AHEAD: Copy the "Bear"y Fun Ways to Make a Memory Scrapbook idea page (page 31) for each girl. Gather scrapbooks from experienced individuals who might be willing to show and tell about scrapbooking ideas.
SCRAPBOOK SHOW-AND-TELL: Review "Bear"y Fun Ways to Make a Memory Scrapbook page, showing an example. Have girls who have done scrapbooks bring pages to show. You could talk about some of the following techniques: matting or cropping, using decorative edged scissors, corner edges, mounting photos, pockets, pop-ups, lettering, die cuts, borders, rubber stamping, paper embossing, etc.

Goal #1 Activity – Create Borders or Designs Using Stencils:

YOU'LL NEED: Copy of goal card and stencils (pages 32-33) for each girl, markers, paper, artist's spray adhesive glue, acrylic or poster paint, sponges, scissors, black marker pen, and a paper punch.
ACTIVITY: See goal card (page 30) for details.

Success Snack – Scrap Happy Sandwich:

1. Cut two slices of bread into a round shape using a Mason jar ring to cut, or cut off crust and corners with a knife.
2. Spread peanut butter and jelly on the bottom slice of bread.
3. Top with the second slice of bread.
4. Using jelly from a decorator tube, create a smile on top of sandwich.
5. Tell girls to be SCRAP HAPPY, to use their imaginations to preserve their memories. Don't wait for the perfect supplies or the perfect time to make their memory book. Preserve your memories as they happen in a scrapbook before they fade.

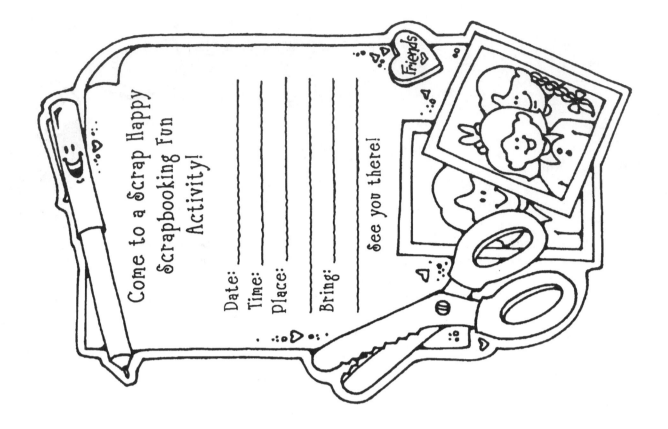

Come to a Scrap Happy
Scrapbooking Fun
Activity!

Date: _____
Time: _____
Place: _____

Bring: _____

See you there!

Achievement Days   Scrap Happy Scrapbook Fun!

FAMILY HISTORY
GOAL #1:
Create Borders or Designs Using Stencils

Once you learn to create borders and designs using stencils, you can make scrapbook borders and even greeting cards.

YOU'LL NEED: Paper, stencil patterns, artist's spray adhesive glue, markers or acrylic or poster paint, sponge, scissors, black marker pen, and a paper punch.

STENCIL STEPS:

1. Cut out stencils on the outside border.

2. Fan-fold stencil strips, cut out stencils, use paper punch to make circles.

3. Using a artist's spray adhesive glue, lightly spray the back of border. Place on page to hold in place.

4. Color where images are cut out with markers, or sponge in paint.

5. Let dry and remove stencil from page. You can reuse stencils if careful.

6. Use a black or dark marker to draw balloon strings, create drawings, or lettering.

7. Use your imagination to create your own stencils and borders.

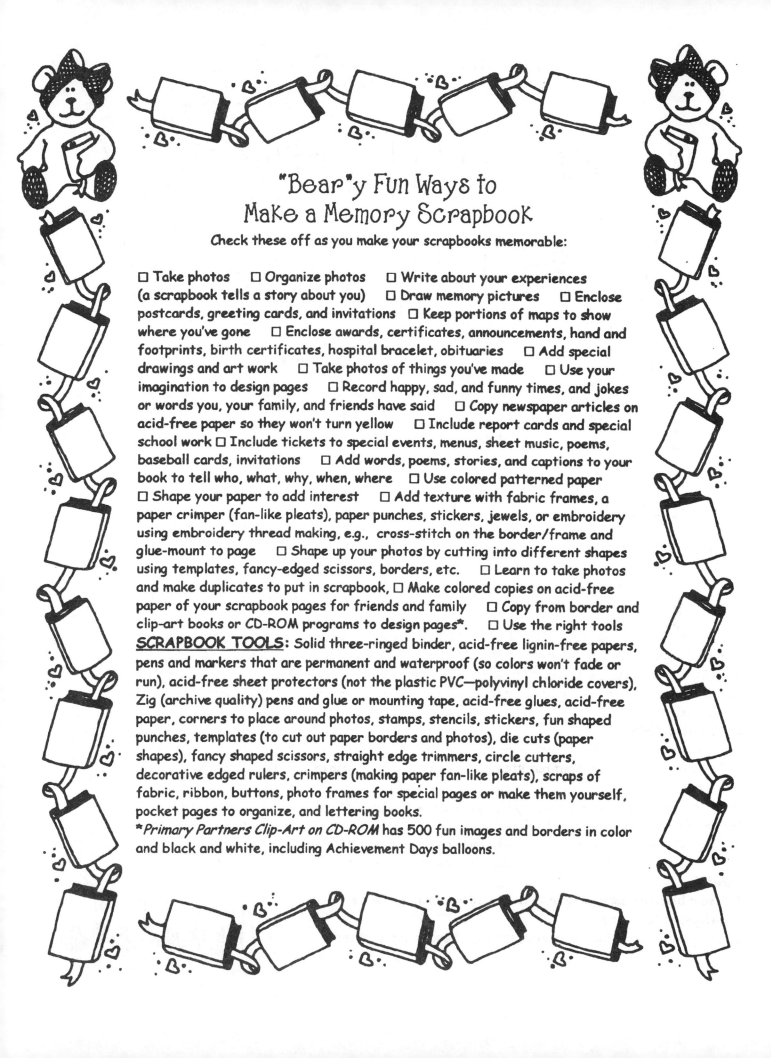

"Bear"y Fun Ways to Make a Memory Scrapbook

Check these off as you make your scrapbooks memorable:

☐ Take photos   ☐ Organize photos   ☐ Write about your experiences (a scrapbook tells a story about you)   ☐ Draw memory pictures   ☐ Enclose postcards, greeting cards, and invitations   ☐ Keep portions of maps to show where you've gone   ☐ Enclose awards, certificates, announcements, hand and footprints, birth certificates, hospital bracelet, obituaries   ☐ Add special drawings and art work   ☐ Take photos of things you've made   ☐ Use your imagination to design pages   ☐ Record happy, sad, and funny times, and jokes or words you, your family, and friends have said   ☐ Copy newspaper articles on acid-free paper so they won't turn yellow   ☐ Include report cards and special school work ☐ Include tickets to special events, menus, sheet music, poems, baseball cards, invitations   ☐ Add words, poems, stories, and captions to your book to tell who, what, why, when, where   ☐ Use colored patterned paper ☐ Shape your paper to add interest   ☐ Add texture with fabric frames, a paper crimper (fan-like pleats), paper punches, stickers, jewels, or embroidery using embroidery thread making, e.g., cross-stitch on the border/frame and glue-mount to page   ☐ Shape up your photos by cutting into different shapes using templates, fancy-edged scissors, borders, etc.   ☐ Learn to take photos and make duplicates to put in scrapbook, ☐ Make colored copies on acid-free paper of your scrapbook pages for friends and family   ☐ Copy from border and clip-art books or CD-ROM programs to design pages*.   ☐ Use the right tools

SCRAPBOOK TOOLS: Solid three-ringed binder, acid-free lignin-free papers, pens and markers that are permanent and waterproof (so colors won't fade or run), acid-free sheet protectors (not the plastic PVC—polyvinyl chloride covers), Zig (archive quality) pens and glue or mounting tape, acid-free glues, acid-free paper, corners to place around photos, stamps, stencils, stickers, fun shaped punches, templates (to cut out paper borders and photos), die cuts (paper shapes), fancy shaped scissors, straight edge trimmers, circle cutters, decorative edged rulers, crimpers (making paper fan-like pleats), scraps of fabric, ribbon, buttons, photo frames for special pages or make them yourself, pocket pages to organize, and lettering books.

Primary Partners Clip-Art on CD-ROM has 500 fun images and borders in color and black and white, including Achievement Days balloons.

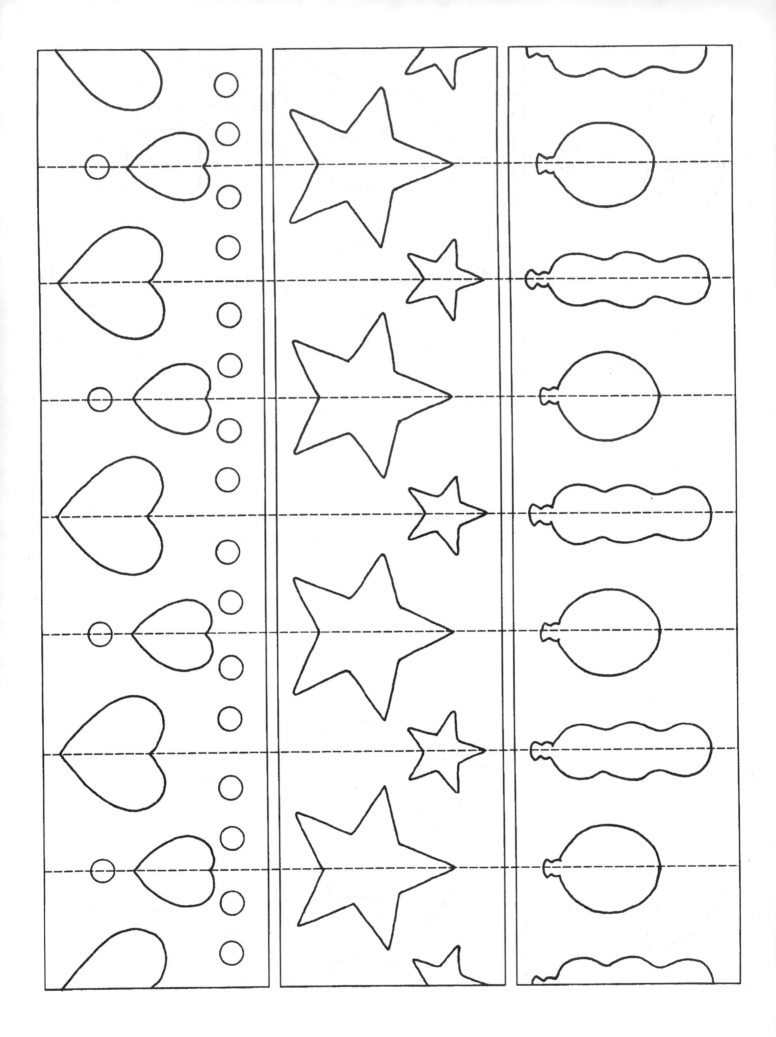

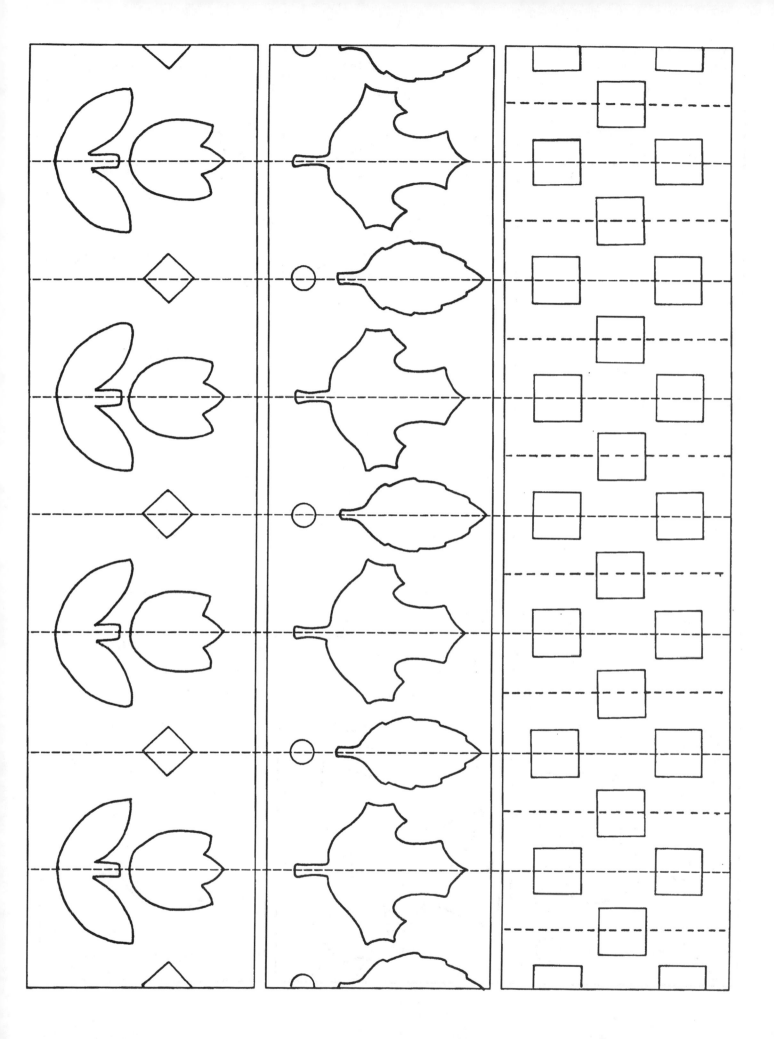

FAMILY HISTORY

Theme #2: "Meet My Ancestor" Spotlight

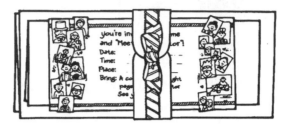

Invitation: Copy-and-create invitation (page 35) to give to girls a week before activity. Include the Spotlight of My Ancestor form (page 36) detailed below*. Also include the goal handout (page 35) showing how to fill out the form.

Icebreaker Activity - Who's Who in My Book of Remembrance:

*Ask girls ahead of time to bring scrapbooks filled with pictures to show-and-tell who is who in several of the pictures. Let each girl show at least one page and tell who these special people are.

Goal #2 Activity - Spotlight My Ancestor:

YOU'LL NEED: Copy of goal card and "Meet My Ancestor" Spotlight (pages 35-36) for each girl.

*Attach the Spotlight of My Ancestor form and the goal handout to the invitation. Invitation asks girls to bring a complete spotlight page of their ancestor. Assemble as shown right: Fold and place the Spotlight of My Ancestor on the bottom, the goal handout in the middle, and the invitation on top. Cut the ribbon and bow from the invitation page and glue the ribbon around the papers and bow on top.

ACTIVITY: See goal card (page 35) for details. Give girls the opportunity to spotlight their ancestors by reading from the form and showing the picture.

Spotlight of **My Ancestor**

By: _____

Name: _____
Born: _____
Place: _____
Married: _____
Spouse: _____
Died: _____
Place: _____

How related? _____
_____
_____

Summary of ancestor's history: _____
_____
_____
_____
_____
_____

Success Snack: Grandma's Cookie Jar Remembrance:

Have girls gather around a jar of homemade cookies labeled: Grandma's Cookie Jar. As you eat, ask them to share what they like and remember about their grandparents. You could even ask each girl ahead of time to bring pictures of their grandparents with a story to tell. After listening to each girl, suggest they go to their grandparents to gather and record their stories. The treasures of firsthand stories that they gather can be passed on; girls can read them to their children, who will pass them on to the next generation.

You're invited to come and "Meet My Ancestor"!

Date: _____

Time: _____

Place: _____

Bring: A completed spotlight page of your ancestor

See you there!

Achievement Days

"Meet My Ancestor" Spotlight

FAMILY HISTORY

GOAL #2:

Spotlight My Ancestor

Using the Spotlight My Ancestor form, write about one of your ancestors, share the story with someone, and place it in your Family History or Book of Remembrance.

TO SPOTLIGHT:

1. Write the name, birth date, place born, marriage date, spouse's name, date and place of death.
2. Write how you were related.
3. Write a summary of your ancestor's history. Use the back of page if needed.
4. Find a photo and place the photo or photocopy of the photo on the page.
5. Bring the page to Achievement Days to share or share with your family at home.

Spotlight of
My Ancestor
By: _____

Name: _____
Born: _____
Place: _____
Married: _____
Spouse: _____
Died: _____
Place: _____

How related? _____
_____

Summary of ancestor's history: _____
_____
_____
_____
_____
_____
_____
_____

Spotlight of My Ancestor

By: _____

Name: _____

Born: _____

Place: _____

Married: _____

Spouse: _____

Died: _____

Place: _____

How related? _____

_____

_____

Summary of ancestor's history: _____

_____

_____

_____

_____

_____

_____

_____

_____

FAMILY SKILLS

Theme #1: Dough Art from the Heart

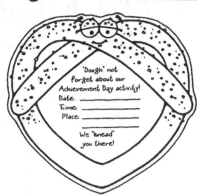

Invitation: Copy-and-create invitation (page 38) to give to girls a week before activity.

Icebreaker Activity – Bread Baking Quiz and Demo:

DO AHEAD: Supply a card and pencil or pen for each girl to take quiz. If possible locate the book *Kids' Ideas with Frozen Dough by Rhodes* from your library or call Rhodes: 1-800-876-7333.

QUIZ: Hand each girl a card and pencil. Ask them to write how to make bread, writing what they imagine the recipe and steps to be. After the demonstration, for a good laugh, leader can read the girl's recipes aloud. You might have some very strange ingredients, along with some crazy directions.

LITTLE RED HEN: Review the old folk tale of "The Little Red Hen" who worked so hard to make the bread. Knowing the steps it takes to make bread, the girls will appreciate every bite.

DOUGH ART FROM THE HEART: Say, "Dough art comes from the heart, because it takes a lot of effort to make homemade bread. This is one way to show your family your love for them, because of the time and energy you spent making something for them to enjoy."

DEMO: For demo, make the BASIC BREAD recipe and make pizza, heart-shaped pretzels, and braid some bread. Have some already raised dough ready to form

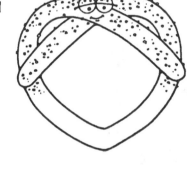

into bread shapes. Tell girls that shaped bread can be frozen on a baking sheet and then placed in a bag for future baking. Once they are frozen loaves won't stick together; but they must be separated before thawing. Place on an oiled pan to raise.

Goal #1 Activity – Create Heart or Other Shaped Bread:

YOU'LL NEED: Copy of goal card and recipe cards (pages 38-39) for each girl.

ACTIVITY: See goal card (page 38) for details. Allow girls to create bread from pre-made dough that has raised and is ready to use. Girls can fan-fold the recipes or cut them to make three cards.

Success Snack Activity: Pizza:

Have girls make individual pizzas and enjoy. The pretzels and braids can be made to take home.

PRETZELS: (1) Roll out a 6" x 6" piece of bread dough. (2) Roll into a long shape. (3) Shape into pretzel shape. (4) Baste with butter and chosen topping: coarse salt, cinnamon and sugar, or Parmesan cheese. (5) Let rise 30 minutes. (6) Bake 15 minutes at 350º oven.

BRAID OR BREADSTICKS: Follow Steps 1-2 above braiding three sticks together or individual bread-sticks.

INGREDIENTS:
Basic Bread dough
butter, coarse salt, cinnamon & sugar, Parmesan cheese

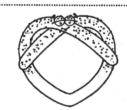

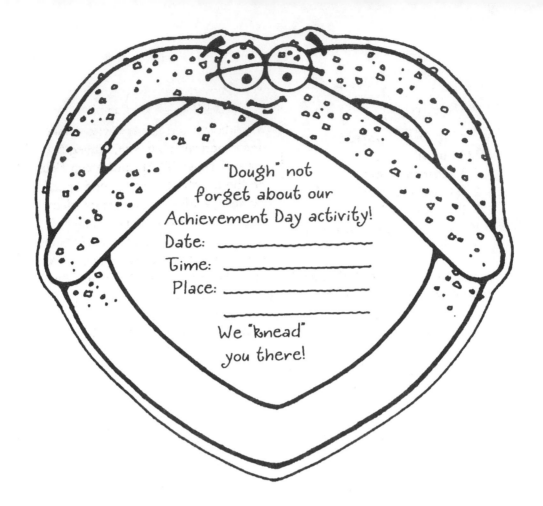

"Dough" not
forget about our
Achievement Day activity!

Date: _____
Time: _____
Place: _____
_____

We "knead"
you there!

Achievement Days

Dough Art from the Heart

FAMILY SKILLS

GOAL #1: Create Heart- or Other-Shaped Bread.

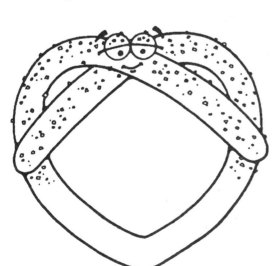

Using the BASIC BREAD recipe make at least one of the following: pizza crust, heart-shaped pretzels, scones, braids, breaded soup bowls by forming and baking bread in small oven safe bowls. Or, use your imagination to make fun bread shapes.

STEPS:
1. Make a BASIC BREAD dough.
2. Let rise.
3. Form into shapes.
4. Let rise again.
5. Bake.

INGREDIENTS:
2 ¼ cups warm water
1/4 cup oil
2 ¼ teaspoons salt
2 ¼ teaspoons sugar
5 ¼ - 6 ½ cups flour
1 tsp. butter (to grease bowl)

BASIC BREAD: (1) Combine the ingredients in a large bowl and mix and knead with a mixer, adding 5 ¼ cups of flour. (2) Spread ¼ cup flour on the countertop and knead bread by hand, adding ½-1 cup more flour if needed. (3) Spread 1 teaspoon soft butter in a clean large bowl. (4) Place dough in buttered bowl and place a clean towel over bowl. (5) Let raise 1-2 hours. (6) Shape into two loaves of bread, 18 rolls, pizza, pretzels, scones, etc. (7) Place shaped dough on oiled pan(s). Cover with a cloth and let raise 30 minutes. (8) Bake rolls at 375° for 16 minutes or bread 40 minutes. TIP: Clean flour off counter with a spatula, cold water, and paper towels.

PIZZA:
1. Preheat oven to 400°.
2. Form raised BASIC BREAD dough into small 6-inch pizzas or small 8-9" pizzas.
3. Form onto cookie sheet or into a pie or round pizza pan.
4. Cover with pizza sauce.
5. Top with grated mozzarella or Monterey Jack cheese.
6. Add the toppings of your choice and bake 400° for 15-20 minutes.

INGREDIENTS:
Basic Bread dough
Pizza sauce
Monterey Jack or mozzarella cheese
Toppings: Grated or chopped pepperoni, cooked sausage, cooked ham, pineapple, green peppers, olives, green onions, mushrooms, and Parmesan cheese.

PRETZELS: (1) Roll out a 6" x 6" piece of bread dough. (2) Roll into a long shape. (3) Shape into pretzel shape. (4) Baste with butter and chosen topping: coarse salt, cinnamon and sugar, or Parmesan cheese. (5) Let rise 30 minutes. (6) Bake 15 minutes at 350° oven.
BRAID OR BREADSTICKS: Follow Steps 1-2 above braiding three sticks together or individual bread-sticks.

INGREDIENTS:
Basic Bread dough
butter, coarse salt, cinnamon & sugar, Parmesan cheese

INGREDIENTS:
2 ½ cups warm water
1/4 cup oil
2 ½ teaspoons salt
2 ½ teaspoons sugar
5 ½ - 6 ½ cups flour
1 tsp. butter (to grease bowl)

BASIC BREAD: (1) Combine the ingredients in a large bowl and mix and knead with a mixer, adding 5 ½ cups of flour. (2) Spread ½ cup flour on the countertop and knead bread by hand, adding ½-1 cup more flour if needed. (3) Spread 1 teaspoon soft butter in a clean large bowl. (4) Place dough in buttered bowl and place a clean towel over bowl. (5) Let dough rise 1-2 hours. (6) Shape into two loaves of bread, 18 rolls, pizza, pretzels, scones, etc. (7) Place shaped dough on oiled pan(s). Cover with a cloth and let rise 30 minutes. (8) Bake rolls at 375º for 16 minutes or bread 40 minutes. TIP: Clean flour off counter with a spatula, cold water, and paper towels.

PIZZA:
1. Preheat oven to 400º.
2. Form raised BASIC BREAD dough into small 6-inch pizzas or small 8-9" pizzas.
3. Form onto cookie sheet or into a pie or round pizza pan.
4. Cover with pizza sauce.
5. Top with grated mozzarella or Monterey Jack cheese.
6. Add the toppings of your choice and bake 400º for 15-20 minutes.

INGREDIENTS:
Basic Bread dough
Pizza sauce
Monterey Jack or
  mozzarella cheese
Toppings: Grated or chopped pepperoni, cooked sausage, cooked ham, pineapple, green peppers, olives, green onions, mushrooms, and Parmesan cheese.

PRETZELS: (1) Roll out a 6" x 6" piece of bread dough. (2) Roll into a long shape. (3) Shape into pretzel shape. (4) Baste with butter and chosen topping: coarse salt, cinnamon and sugar, or Parmesan cheese. (5) Let rise 30 minutes. (6) Bake 15 minutes at 350º oven.
BRAID OR BREADSTICKS: Follow Steps 1-2 above braiding three sticks together or individual bread-sticks.

INGREDIENTS:
Basic Bread dough
butter, coarse salt, cinnamon & sugar, Parmesan cheese

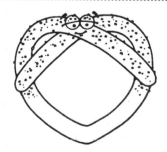

FAMILY SKILLS
Theme #2: Sparkle and Shine!

Invitation: Copy-and-create invitation (page 41) to give to girls a week before activity. If you want girls to bring their own jars, write on the invitation: "Bring a canning pint or quart jar, with lid."

Icebreaker Activity:
Sparkle and Shine Demo

DO AHEAD: Ask a cleaning expert or experts to come and teach girls how to do the jobs found on the job wordstrips (pages 42-45). Have cleaning supplies ready as you go from job to job to complete five or more tough tasks (e.g. cleaning the toilet). Use a broom to clear cobwebs, clean out a drawer, wash a window, dust, clean the sink or faucet with a toothbrush, iron a shirt, and use an SOS or a sponge with scouring pad attached (e.g., wet sponge or cloth, add detergent, scour, and wipe with wet sponge.)

ACTIVITY:

1. Have cleaning expert tell how he/she makes a room or home sparkle and shine.
2. Have the expert show techniques, e.g., those listed above or on the job wordstrips.
3. Have the girls tell how they make their home sparkle and shine.
4. Sing together the song, "This Little Light of Mine" using the words, "This little home of mine, I'm going to let it shine."

Goal #2 Activity: Make a Sparkle and Shine Job Jar and Do Five Jobs

YOU'LL NEED: Copy of goal card (page 41), job jar label and job wordstrips (pages 42-45) on colored cardstock paper, a bottle (to glue label on) for each girl, markers, glue, scissors. Cut out a piece of fabric from the pattern (page 44) and follow directions.
ACTIVITY: See goal card (page 41) for details.

Success Snack: Sparkle and Shine Jello.
Make up some sparkling clear Jello according to directions. As girls eat, talk to girls about how nice it is when a room is sparkling clean. It makes the house look brand new.

You're invited to come and learn how to "Sparkle and Shine"!

Date: _____

Time: _____

Place: _____

See you there!

FAMILY SKILLS

GOAL #2: Create a Sparkle and Shine Job Jar and Do Five Jobs

Make a Sparkle and Shine Job Jar and fill with jobs. Then draw at least five jobs from the jar and complete them.

TO MAKE JOB JAR:
1. Glue the Sparkle and Shine Job Jar label on a jar or enclose the label in a plastic bag.
2. Cut up jobs strips or have your parents create some jobs to place in the jar.
3. Work with your family each day to make your home sparkle and shine!

This little home of mine, I'm gonna let it shine!

This little home of mine, I'm gonna let it shine!

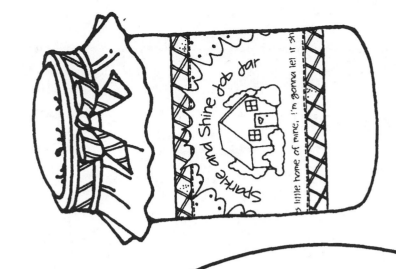

Sparkle and Shine Job Jar

little home of mine, I'm gonna let it sh

Job Jar Fabric Lid Pattern

1. Cut out your choice of fabric using this pattern. Option: Cut out using pinking shears for a zigzag edge.

2. Using 5 to 6 cotton balls for cushion, hot glue in place in the center of the lid.

3. Position fabric over the lid making sure it is centered. Around the edge of the lid, hot glue in a couple places to secure the fabric. Push fabric lid into bottle ring and fix gathers so they evenly surround the lid.

4. Put the lid on the bottle and screw into place. Tie a 20-inch ribbon around the bottle ring and hot glue if desired.

Dust an entire room.		Clean one toilet inside and out.	
Shine two mirrors.		Wash all light-switch covers.	
Dust all pictures in the house.		Empty the trash in three rooms.	
Wash mopboards in one room.		5-minute cleanup on 4 rooms.	
Clean two windows.		Wash sinkful or batch of dishes.	
Wipe off five window sills.		Put 25 things away.	
Wash all doorknobs.		Sweep all the floors.	
Sweep the front and back steps.		Mop the bathroom floor.	
Vacuum all the stairs.		Fold & put away 3 batches of laundry.	

Clean all sinks in house.	Iron for 30 minutes.
Sweep and vacuum entry.	Clean and organize a drawer.
Straighten all clothes in a closet.	Wash all the spice containers.
Clean a closet shelf.	Shake all the rugs.
Shine three pairs of shoes.	Help make a plan for family's work.
Sweep one-half of the garage.	Shine one shelf in refrigerator.
Clear a cluttered countertop.	Find and match all odd socks.
Clean & organize under a sink.	Help Mom or Dad for 30 minutes.
Unload and load the dishwasher.	Polish a piece of furniture.

HEALTH & GROOMING
Theme #1: Beauty Shop Hair Talk

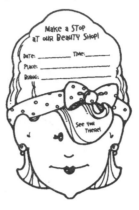

Invitation: Copy-and-create invitation (page 47) to give to girls a week before activity. Ask girls to bring hairstyling accessories, magazines, and tools.

Icebreaker Activity:
Beauty Shop Style Talk

DO AHEAD: Gather several hair styling magazines to find the latest styles. Ask several stylish young women to talk to girls about how they style their hair and use hair accessories.

ACTIVITY: Have young women talk to the girls, look through magazines, and share hairstyling tips. Show books with great ideas (for example, *Hair Styling Tips and Tricks for Girls,* by American Girl Library).

STYLING IDEAS: (1) For knots, create a ponytail or pigtails, braid, twist into a knot and pin down. (2) For buns, make a high ponytail, twist ponytail tightly, and wrap around ponytail elastic; pin bun in place with hairpins or bobby pins. (3) or pigtails, use 3-4 colored elastics going down each pigtail, braid then loop pigtails. (4) To create crown twists, part hair into five sections at the crown; twist and clip sections off with mini clips. (5) For zigzag part, see details on goal instruction card. (6) Straighten hair. (7) Spiral curls. (8) French braid. (9) Braids. (10) Twists.

HAIR ACCESSORIES: jeweled bobby pins, jaw clips, fat and skinny scrunchies, barrettes, bands (elastic, plastic, or metal; some with teeth to grip thin hair), shoe laces, ribbons, twist ties, silk cord or leather shoe laces to tie hair, Velcro stick-ons, and tiny ponytail elastics.

GOAL #1: Learn to Care for and Style Your Hair

YOU'LL NEED: Copy of goal card (page 47), Beauty Shop Hair Talk, My Best Hair Styles, and Find Your Face Shape (pages 48-50) for each girl, pencils, ruler, and markers.

ACTIVITY:

1. Review the Beauty Shop Hair Talk ideas to learn to care for and style your hair.

2. Review the Find Your Face Shape information to help girls determine their face shape and learn how to style their hair to balance their face shape.

3. Tape your face shape against a window. Place the My Best Hairstyles! page over the face shape and trace it onto each of the four squares.

4. Draw in your best hairstyles to balance and flatter your face shape.

Success Snack: Potato Salad Face with Carrot Curls

Serve potato salad on a large plate, forming an oval face shape. Use a potato peeler to shave carrot curls off carrots to create hair, and other vegetables to create face (cucumber eyes, olive nose, and tomato lips).

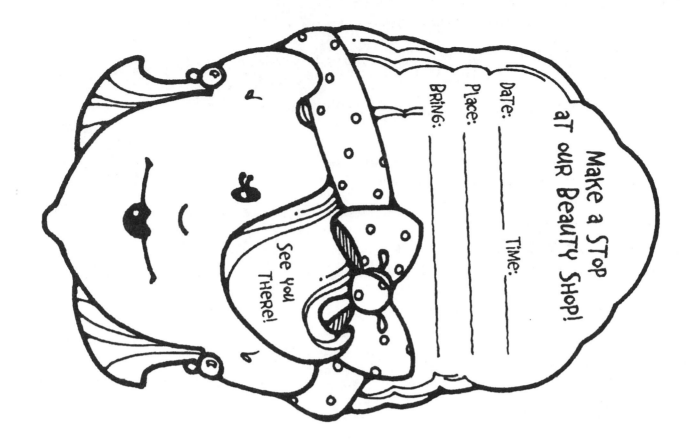

Make a STOP
aT ouR BeauTY SHOP!

Date: _____ Time: _____

Place: _____

BRiNG: _____

See you
THERE!

Achievement Days   Beauty Shop Hair Talk

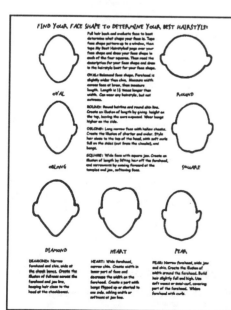

HEALTH & GROOMING

GOAL #1: <u>Learn to Care for and Style Your Hair</u>

Learn to care for and style your own hair:

• Read Beauty Shop Hair Talk ideas to learn to care for and style your hair.

• Determine your face shape and learn how to style your hair to make the most of your face shape.

• Trace your face shape onto My Best Hairstyles! form.

• Design hairstyles that are best for your face shape.

BEAUTY SHOP HAIR TALK

Wash hair daily to smell fresh and clean, and give hair body. Condition to shine.

WHAT TYPE OF HAIR DO YOU HAVE?

TOO THICK: Comb through hair in the shower after applying conditioner to untangle. Use mousse to control frizz. Avoid gels and sprays that add body. Use light hair spray, spraying only the ends, not the roots. Have layered cuts instead of blunt.

IF TOO THICK AND WAVY: Straighten by using a flat brush, pulling it as you blow dry. To curl with a curling iron, go through the hair once to warm the hair, and then a second time, curling only the ends. If hair won't bend, lightly spray water or detangler (leave-in-conditioning spray) before curling. Keep hair medium length or shorter as too much length weighs down the hair, making your hair bottom heavy, taking away fullness on the top. If wearing hair long, layer it around the face.

CURLY HAIR: Use a diffuser to keep curls soft. Comb out to the style you want when hair is set, then dry, pushing diffuser into curls, lifting up. If you want it straightened, a perm solution can be applied to your hair, combing it to pull out the curls.

THIN HAIR: Blow dry bending over, with head upside down, to give volume, then stand up and style normally. Curl hair with a curling iron, using with a smaller curling iron where more lift is needed; where more fullness is needed, spray amplifying hair spray in at the roots rather than on the ends.

HAIR STYLING TIPS FROM A HAIRDRESSER

SHAMPOO AND CONDITION: Use shampoo on the scalp only, not the ends of hair. Use a dime's worth of shampoo for the first shampoo. Rinse, then shampoo again. Condition. **TO BLOW DRY:** Towel dry first. Comb through. Pin individual curls up with clamps. Blow dry the bottom curls, working up, using a round, soft-bristle brush. The longer the hair, the bigger the brush should be. If blow drying hair without using clips, bend over and dry roots, then stand up to dry the top of head.

DON'T OVER DRY HAIR: Towel dry and comb through hair, curving the ends to the style you want (up or down). Then let air dry 15 minutes before blow drying. Use a spray or leave-in conditioner on hair before using a curling iron.

TO CURL UP: After blow drying, pin individual curls on top with clamps. Curl the bottom curls first, working to the top. To use a curling iron, practice first with a cool iron. The best way is to practice with a cool iron without looking in a mirror to get the feel of it. Iron temperature should not be too hot or you can burn your hair. For longer-lasting curl, go through the hair strand once with the hot iron, then go through the same strand again, holding the curl in place longer. Remember, professional curling irons are hotter than discount store irons.

FIND YOUR FACE SHAPE TO DETERMINE YOUR BEST HAIRSTYLE:

OVAL

Pull hair back and evaluate face to best determine what shape your face is. Tape face shape pattern up to a window, then tape My Best Hairstyles! page over your face shape and draw your face shape in each of the four squares. Then read the description for your face shape and draw in the hairstyle best for your face shape.

OVAL: Balanced face shape. Forehead is slightly wider than chin. Measure width across face at brow, then measure length. Length is 1½ times longer than width. Can wear any hairstyle, but not extreme.

ROUND: Round hairline and round chin line. Create an illusion of length by giving height on the top, leaving the ears exposed. Wear bangs higher on the side.

OBLONG: Long narrow face with hallow cheeks. Create the illusion of shorter and wider. Style hair close to the top of the head, with soft curls full on the sides (out from the cheeks), and bangs.

SQUARE: Wide face with square jaw. Create an illusion of length by lifting hair off the forehead, and narrowness by coming forward at the temples and jaw, softening face.

ROUND

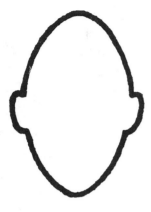

OBLONG

SQUARE

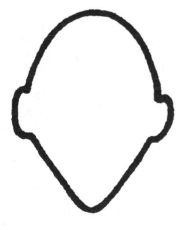

DIAMOND

HEART

PEAR

DIAMOND: Narrow forehead and chin, wide at the cheek bones. Create the illusion of fullness across the forehead and jaw line, keeping hair close to the head at the cheekbones.

HEART: Wide forehead, narrow chin. Create width in lower part of face and decrease the width on the forehead. Create a part with bangs flipped up or slanted to one side, adding width or softness at jaw line.

PEAR: Narrow forehead, wide jaw and chin. Create the illusion of width around the forehead. Build hair slightly full and high. Use soft waves or semi-curl, covering part of the forehead. Widen forehead with curls.

MY BEST HAIRSTYLES!

HEALTH & GROOMING

Theme #2: Healthy Food Fun

Invitation: Copy-and-create invitation (page 52) to give girls a week before activity.

Icebreaker Activities: Wrong Choice Wilma Card Game and Good Choice Food Demo

DO AHEAD: Copy four sets of cards, one Wrong-Choice Wilma card, and rules (pages 53-55) on colored cardstock paper. (Or print colored cards from CD-ROM on white cardstock paper.) Cut out cards. Make an extra set for each girl to take home (optional). Get food ready for the Food Prep Demo.

WRONG CHOICE WILMA CARD GAME: Play the game, following the instructions (page 53).

FOOD PREP DEMO IDEAS: (1) Show how to prepare healthy foods, e.g., washing fruits and vegetables, cutting them up, cooking, etc. (2) Show how to use a knife, a potato and carrot peeler, apple corer, grader, food processor, etc. (3) Show how to cut up a fresh pineapple and how to break up cauliflower and broccoli to make florets (rather than cutting them up). (4) Show how to cook and prepare spaghetti squash and other kinds of squash. (5) Show how to cook frozen vegetables. (6) Show how to cook pasta, adding vegetables and a sauce. (6) Talk about junk food as high calorie/empty nutrition foods. Because they are low in nutrition, your body craves more food than needed, causing weight gain.

GOAL #2: Tic-Tac-Toe In the Know Diet Game

YOU'LL NEED: Copy of goal card (page 52) and the Tic-Tac-Toe In-the-Know Diet Game (page 56) for each girl.

ACTIVITY: For details see the goal card and Tic-Tac-Toe In-the-Know Diet Game (page 52).

Success Snack: Salad or Baked Potato Bar

Assign each girl the task of preparing items for salad or baked potato bar. Bake potatoes ahead 400° for 1 hour (wrapped in foil). Show girls how to bake a potato in the microwave 8-9 minutes (adding 1 tsp. water in bowl and covering with clear wrap).

SALAD BAR IDEAS: Lettuce, cucumbers, garbanzo and kidney beans, pineapple, cherry tomatoes, salad dressing, olives, red onions, sunflower seeds, etc.

BAKED POTATO BAR IDEAS: Baked potatoes, sour cream, grated cheese, chili, cooked broccoli or vegetables.

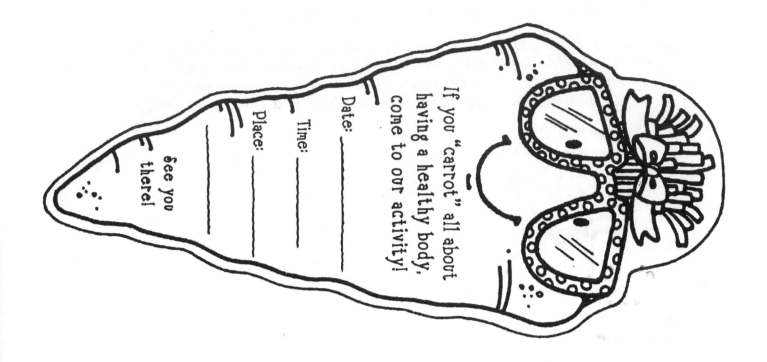

If you "carrot" all about
having a healthy body,
come to our activity!

Date:

Time:

Place:

See you
there!

Achievement Days   Healthy Food Fun

HEALTH & GROOMING

TIC-TAC-TOE IN-THE-KNOW DIET GAME:

Record your diet moves each day on the game boards below. Enter your moves as you eat. Place an X after
eating a healthy food and an O after eating junk food. If you make more X moves, before the O moves
take over, you win! You win if you make three Xs in a vertical, horizontal, or diagonal line.

THE moves you MAKE DETERMINE HOW you LOOK AND FEEL.

SUNDAY

MONDAY

TUESDAY

WEDNESDAY

THURSDAY

FRIDAY

SATURDAY

NOTES:

GOAL #2:

**Play the Tic-Tac-Toe
In-the-Know Diet Game**

Play the Tic-Tac-Toe In-the-Know Diet Game for a
week to remind you how you are eating. See rules on
game board.

HEALTH FOOD DEFINITION: Fruits and vegetables,
high fiber grains, 100% fruit juices, meat, chicken, fish,
eggs, milk, sour cream, cheese, yogurt, tofu, soy
products, e.g., soy milk, soy cheese, soy sour cream, and
soy cream cheese, fruit based popsicles.

JUNK FOOD DEFINITION: Low in nutrition and fiber,
high in sugar, starch, salt, and fat. Examples: cake,
cookies, doughnuts, chips, breads, pasta, and muffins
with refined flour instead of whole grain, high
sugar/low fiber cereals, soda pop, chocolate, candy, ice
cream, sherbet, sugar based popsicles.

TIC-TAC-TOE IN-THE-KNOW DIET GAME:

Record your diet moves each day on the game boards below. Enter your moves as you eat. Place an X after eating a healthy food and an O after eating junk food. If you make more X moves, before the O moves take over, you win! You win if you make three Xs in a vertical, horizontal, or diagonal line.

THE MOVES YOU MAKE DETERMINE HOW YOU LOOK AND FEEL.

WEDNESDAY

THURSDAY

SUNDAY

FRIDAY

MONDAY

TUESDAY

SATURDAY

NOTES:

Wrong-Choice Wilma

WRONG CHOICE WILMA
Card Game:
Play this game like Old Maid.

1. Start with a deck of 49 cards (four of each card, plus one Wrong-Choice Wilma card). Cards are listed below*.

2. The object is to gather pairs of healthy food cards (for example, two Ana Banana or two Frieda Fish cards) and get rid of all the cards in your hand without getting stuck with Wrong-Choice Wilma.

3. Deal out all the cards to the girls (some will have more than others).

4. Players look at their hand and place any pairs face up in front of them.

5. Players take turns pulling one card from the hand of the player on their right. If card matches one in the player's hand, she adds it to the other matched pairs in front of her.

6. Play until all the cards have been paired up and discarded. The player left with the unmatched Wrong-Choice Wilma card is the loser.

NOTE: As cards are matched up and discarded, name the card by saying the healthy choice girl's name (like Cutie Cucumber or Ana Banana).

*CARDS: Wrong-Choice Wilma, Mille Melon, Ana Banana, Keri Strawberry, Pippy Pepper, Ada Apple, Cutie Cucumber, Frieda Fish, Chicky Chicken, Tanya Tomato, Lucy Lettuce, Rita Wheata Bread, Valery Celery.

Copy 4 for each set of cards.

Millie Melon

Ana Banana

Keri Strawberry

Pippy Pepper

Ada Apple

Cutie Cucumber

Copy 4 for each set of cards.

Frieda Fish

Chicky Chicken

Tanya Tomato

Lucy Lettuce

Rita Wheata Bread

Valery Celery

HOSPITALITY

Theme #1: Mending and Keeping a Friendship

Invitation: Copy-and-create invitation (page 58) to give girls a week before activity.

Icebreaker Activity:
Friendship Flash Card Sneak Preview

DO AHEAD: Copy the Friendship Flash Cards (pages 59-60) on cardstock paper for each girl. Cut out one set as an example and place in the Friendship First-Aid Kit (see below).

ACTIVITY: Help girls learn ways to mend a friendship or keep a friendship going. Hide the flash cards around a room and have girls search for them to share friendship tips. The cards can be placed in the Friendship First-Aid kit (detailed below).

Goal #1 Activity: Make a Friendship First-Aid Kit

YOU'LL NEED: Copy of (1) goal card with instructions on how to make Kit, (2) Friendship First-Aid Kit labels, (3) postcards, and (4) friendship gift tags (pages 58, 61-63) for each girl. You'll also need a file folder for each girl, scissors, markers, paper punch, yarn or ribbon.

ACTIVITY: Make a Friendship First-Aid Kit. See goal card (page 58) for details.

Success Snack: Heart-Shaped Cookies

Have sugar cookie dough ready to cut out hearts, large and small. Bake and decorate. Tell girls that the heart represents hospitality and friendship. When we show our love to others unconditionally (without expecting friendship in return), we will always have friends. Start by being a friend to yourself.

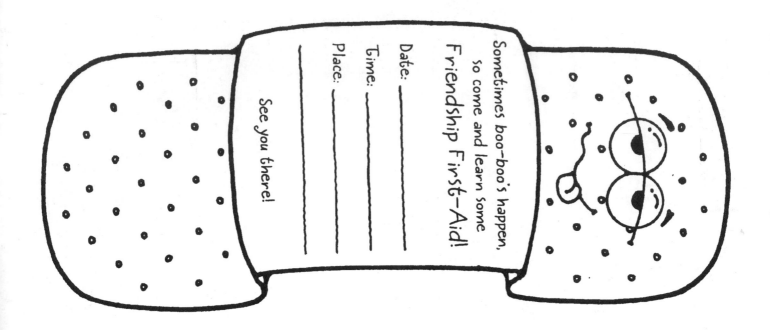

Sometimes boo-boo's happen, so come and learn some
Friendship First-Aid!

Date: _____
Time: _____
Place: _____

See you there!

HOSPITALITY

GOAL #1: Make a Friendship First-Aid Kit

Use this kit to store ideas and tools for patching up a broken friendship or keeping a friendship going. Include postcards to send to a friend, gift tags to attach to friendship gifts, and friendship flash cards to remind you of ways to be a friend. Use kit to store greeting cards, thank-you cards, and so on.

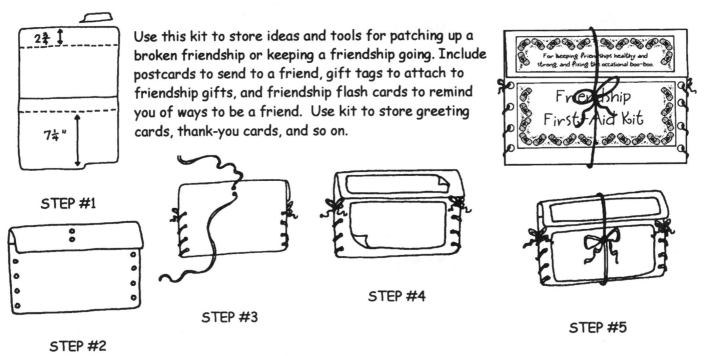

STEP #1

STEP #2

STEP #3

STEP #4

STEP #5

TO MAKE KIT: <u>Step #1</u>: Using a letter-size file folder, trim off the tab so edge is smooth. <u>Step #2</u>: Punch holes on the sides and top as shown, punching through both layers. <u>Step #3</u>: Sew string or ribbon through the holes on both sides, and tie. <u>Step #4</u>: Color, cut out, and glue on the Friendship First-Aid Kit labels (smallest label at top of flap and larger label below). <u>Step #5</u>: Thread three feet of string or ribbon through back holes. Wrap string around and tie in front.

Stand up
for a
friend.

Help your
friend to
make correct
decisions.

Take time
to listen
to a friend.

Apologize
quickly if you
have hurt
your friend's
feelings.

Forgive and
forget when
a friend has
offended you.

Rejoice in
your friend's
successes.

Don't ever
gossip about
your friends.

Compliment
or praise
your friend.

Never criticize a friend.

Learn all about your friend's favorite things: food, color, movie, etc.

Invite your friend to join your conversations with other friends.

Invite your friend to activities with your other friends.

Do little acts of service to let your friend know you care.

Help your friend with chores and projects.

Invite your friend to your house and introduce her to your family.

Be honest and trustworthy.

For keeping friendships healthy and strong, and fixing the occasional boo-boo.

Friendship
First-Aid Kit

As a friend, you shine!

To:

When I'm in a jam, I'm "berry" glad to have a friend like you.

To:

You leave me in stitches!

To:

Friends like you don't swim along every day!

to:

Bag of popcorn

I'm not just trying to butter you up, but,...

...you sure pop up when I need a Friend!

Banana or banana bread

As a friend, you're mighty appealing!

Loaf of bread

Sorry to hear you're feeling crumb-y. Get well soon!

When life's got me licked, it helps to have a friend like you!

Sucker

Roll of SweetTarts candy

Your heart's in the right spot!

Package of M&M's

You're a Mighty Marvelous and friend!

HOSPITALITY
Theme #2: It's Party Time!

Invitation: Copy-and-create invitation (page 65) to give girls a week before activity.

Icebreaker Activity:
Learn How to Plan a Fun Party

YOU'LL NEED: Copy of Goal #2 goal card (page 65), It's Party Time! book, and It's Party Time Party Planner (pages 66-68) for each girl, scissors, stapler, pencils, and party books.

PARTY PREP MEETING (two weeks ahead):

Step #1: Make and review the It's Party Time! book to learn ways to have a fun party. Color, cut out, and staple book together.

Step #2: Review the It's Party Time! Party Planner.

Step #3: Decide on a party theme.

Step #4: Divide into groups, and assign each group their part in the party plans: invitations, decorations, games, activities, crafts, favors, and treats. Have each group secretly tell you their plans for the party. Suggest they make their plans inexpensive, using items they may have on hand at home to contribute. Girls could also announce what they need to the group to see if others could supply any items needed. Tell them they can use what they have at home and say, "You don't need to spend a lot of money to have fun." Have a budget for food and balloons.

Step #5: Follow up during the next two weeks, before the party to make sure invitations are delivered and the party is ready.

Step #6: Help girls make the treats and decorate the day before.

HAVE THE PARTY to Complete the Achievement Days Goal #2:

Goal #2 Activity: Enjoy a Fun Party

ACTIVITY: Now that you have gone through Steps #1-6 party planning steps (above) two weeks before, do your part to put on a fun party, then evaluate the party afterwards. See goal card (page 65) for details.

Success Snack: Party Treat for Prep Time

(two-weeks before party). Make cupcakes and frost, topping with gumdrops to look like balloons, and adding balloon streamers with frosting in a tube. Make a Muddy Buddies party mix: Mix together peanuts, candy-coated chocolate candies, chocolate-covered peanuts, raisins, and a cracker snack mix, e.g., wheat germ nuts snack, or Chex cereal mix. Drizzle dry-fast chocolate syrup (found in ice cream toppings) over the top and mix together.

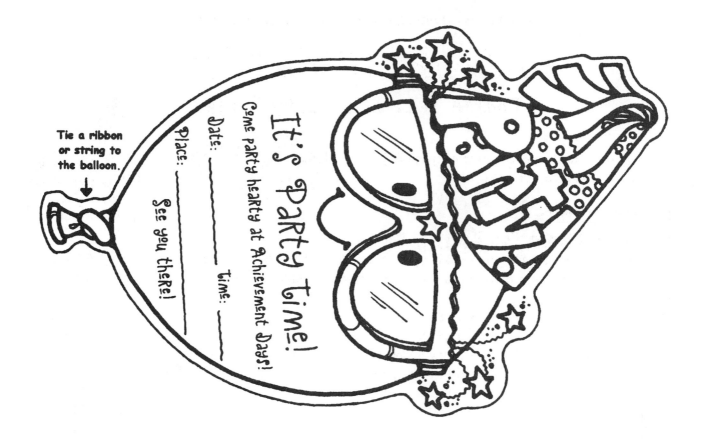

Tie a ribbon or string to the balloon.

It's Party Time!

Come party hearty at Achievement Days!

Date: _____

Place: _____ Time: _____

See you there!

HOSPITALITY

GOAL #2: Plan and Have a Fun Party

It's Party Time!

How to Plan a Fun Party!

With your Achievement Days friends, use the It's Party Time! book and party planner (shown left and right) to plan and have a fun party.
1. Select party theme.
2. Divide into groups, assigning the following: invitations, decorations, games and activities, crafts, favors and prizes, and treats.

It's Party Time!
Party Planner

Friends to Invite	Invitation Details
	Theme: _____
	Date: _____
	Time: _____
	Place: _____
	Bring: _____
Decorations	**Games & Activities**
Crafts & Favors	**Treats**

It's Party time!

How to Plan a fun Party!

Invitations:

1. Choose a party theme.
2. Allow enough time to plan the party (at least 2-3 weeks).
3. Calendar your plans with day-to-day tasks.
4. Enlist help of friends and family.
5. Design your invitation to match your theme; be creative as you design invitations (have a pop-up invitation or attach an item or treat to invite that matches the party's theme. Use stickers that match theme, too.
6. Include the following in your invitation: date, time, place, and theme. Note if it's a birthday party and list items to bring if any. With birthday parties, guestsl bring gifts (but don't ask them to bring treats).
7. Write R.S.V.P. at the end and your phone number if you wish them to respond, by letting you know if they can attend. If you want them to respond by a certain date, write "R.S.V.P. by such-and-such date."
8. Deliver invitation a week or two in advance. Call friends who live a distance away and whose invitations are mailed, telling them the invitation has been sent.

Decorations:

Set the mood with theme-matching decorations.

1. Balloons always add excitement and can be used in games and as favors to take home. Tie to back of chairs, or hang from the ceiling, light, or stairs.
2. Streamers hung in the room create atmosphere.
3. Images that represent the party theme can be hung from streamers.
4. Welcome banners and signs create the mood.
5. Autograph posters decorate while they invite friends to sign their name and write comments.
6. Table decorations can be created using plain plates cups, utensils, and table cloth. Use your imagination to decorate these and create a centerpiece that matches the theme.
7. Scatter confetti and streamers on the table.
8. Use favors as table decorations.
9. Use food to decorate the table.
10. Use photos, posters, or travel brochures.
11. Create mobiles by hanging objects from the ceiling or hangers.

games:

Learn basic games and use your imagination to create your own version of each game. Pin the Tail on the Donkey could be Pin the Nose on the Clown, and Musical Chairs could become Musical Mummies.

1. Go to the library and study game books. Choose those that fit the party theme.
2. Write down each game step-by-step.
3. Make a list of supplies needed for each game.
4. Have game supplies and notes in a container, keeping all game supplies ready to use.
5. Make a list of which game you will play first, second, just before you eat, just before guests open gifts, just before guests go home. Remember that quieter games should be played just before you eat or before guests go home.
6. Give each game a certain time limit, but continue the game if guests are having a great time. Discontinue games that seem to drag.
7. Try games out on your family and close friends before the party.
8. Make sure that you explain the game rules clearly.
9. Be spontaneous when guests come up with a fun game of their own, then return to your party plans.

Activities:

Activities are fun and can be a welcome change from games. FUN IDEAS:

1. As guests arrive, give each one a card with their name written at the top. Pin it on their back and hand them a pencil. Ask guests to write a secret message on each guest's card. Read them at the end of the party.

2. Give each guest five small safety pins to pin on their clothing. Ask them to ask certain questions of the other guests. Those who don't answer within five seconds lose a pin. The one with the most pins at the end of the party wins a prize.

3. Have an entertainer come or have a talent show.

4. Write mixed-up sentences on a piece of paper that relate to the theme. Have guests unscramble the sentences. The first to get all of them right wins!

5. Design a maze on a place mat at the table. When guests eat have them complete the maze. The first to get through wins!

6. Birthday gifts can be fun to open if the guests first hide them in one or two rooms. Then the birthday girl or boy has to find them to open them.

Crafts:

Crafts become a fun activity where guests can make something to take home or decorate their own plates, cups, spoons, straws, or napkins. There are different types of crafts to enjoy.

FOOD CRAFTS: • decorate a giant cookie, cake, or cupcakes • animal cracker farm with graham cracker barn (use frosting and candies) • silly sandwiches, cutting meat, bread, and cheeses with cookie cutters and decorating the top with cheese from the tube • baking bread shapes • Lifesaver or candy bar car • wormy dirt (crushed Oreo cookies) with gummy worms • inside-out sandwiches • no-bake cookies (roll peanut butter or sweetened cream cheese in shredded coconut or crushed peanuts)

MISCELLANEOUS CRAFTS: • sun catchers • hats • pressed flowers • safety pin or paper-clip bracelet • blue jean tote bag • illustrate your own story book • decorate visors or hats • magnets • rock painting • puppet theater • melt/remold crayons • stationery • bird feeder with plastic bottle • make gift wrap • beads • clay • play dough • collage • fabric fun • finger paints • hats • masks • puppets • kites • paper bag designs • paper plate designs • foam fun • mobile • tole painting • sponge painting • frames

Favors and Prizes:

Favors, prizes, and goodie bags make an impression during and at the end of the party.

FAVOR IDEAS: • puppet • scarf • paper flowers • artwork • decorated bandannas • baseball cap • goldfish • ladybug • pumpkin • toothbrush • painted rock • T-shirt • chalk • masks • decorated glasses • wristbands or bracelets • hair accessories • belts • jewelry • decorated pillow case • photo and frame • decorated candle

GAME PRIZES: • animal crackers • popcorn ball • balloon • stickers • glasses • basket • potpourri or sachets • cookie cutter • sewing repair kit • nail polish • candy bar • colored paper clips • fan • lip gloss • fake spider or worm • miniature dice • Old Maid or Fish game • ball • toys • candy kisses • bubble solution • stuffed animal • comic strip or joke • bookmark • seed packet • poem • song

GOODIE BAG IDEAS: Fill goodie bags half full of paper grass or popcorn, unless the favors and prizes fill the bag. Then fill with treats and favors:
• lollipop • cookie • licorice rope • gummy worms, fish, candy • candy bars • small container drinks

Treats:

Guests can be asked to bring treats, unless it's a birthday party. Serve treats in different ways:

(1) Walk-About Treats: Snacks for guests to munch on during the party. If serving a meal or dessert, provide plates for them to serve themselves.

(2) Sit Down Treats: Guests don't eat until it's time for the meal, sitting down at the table to be served.

(3) Sack Lunch Treats: Serve a sack lunch sitting on a blanket indoors or outdoors. The bag could be decorated and become the take-home goodie bag, filling the bag as guests leave. Write names on bags.

(4) Treasure Hunt Treats: Have guests search for clues to find their treats.

(5) Show-Time Snacks: While watching a movie, a play or a talent show, serve snacks in bowls, e.g., popcorn, party mixes, cheese and crackers, chips and dips, licorice or suckers.

(6) Healthy Snacks: Fruit and vegetables can be cut up in interesting ways to make an impression.

It's Party time!
Party Planner

Friends to Invite

Invitation Details

Theme: _____
Date: _____
Time: _____
Place: _____
_____
Bring: _____
_____

Decorations

Games & Activities

Crafts & Favors

Treats

OUTDOOR FUN & SKILLS
Theme #1: Splish Splash Water Fun & Safety

Invitation: Copy-and-create invitation (page 70) to give girls a week before activity. If going to a swimming pool, name location and ask them to bring their suit.

Icebreaker Activity:
Review Water Safety Rules and Fun Water Activities

DO AHEAD: Copy the Splish Splash Water Fun activities (pages 71-72) two sided, or glue the two pages back-to-back. Color and laminate for splish splash durability.

LEARN DON'T SINK WATER SAFETY: Review the following rules for water safety (also on goal card).

1. Always swim with a friend.
2. Don't swim where it is too deep for your ability.
3. If the surf's up, wait until the water is safe; don't swim near ocean waves unless with an adult and you are an experienced swimmer.
4. Dive only into water where you know it is not shallow or rocky, clear of other swimmers.
5. Stay away from boats and water skiers.
6. Never swim in unfamiliar water; at first walk out and swim back in.
7. If using inflatable tubes, be careful not to drift out too far from shore.
8. If playing deep water games or when you're in a boat, always wear a fitted life jacket.

GOAL #1 Activity: Learn Water Safety Rules and Fun Water Activities

YOU'LL NEED: Copy of goal card (page 70) and Splish Splash Water Fun Activities (pages 71-72) for each girl.

ACTIVITY (see goal card (page 70) for a list of activities. Present the activities in a pool. Or, if a pool is not available, have girls go through the motions so that when they are in the water, they can take their list and enjoy!

Success Snack: Gummy Fish in Jello

Cups. For a cool-off treat, serve blue Jello filled with gummy fish, topped with a whipped cream cloud. Serve with a plastic spoon. Tell girls that in order to keep afloat, they must learn how to swim safely.

TO MAKE: Make a 3-ounce package of blueberry Jello and pour into the bottom of a clear plastic cup (filling half full), adding gummy fish, e.g., Sharks, or Swedish fish (or other flat gummy candies). Refrigerate 30-40 minutes. Make a second box of Jello to fill cup. Refrigerate until firm. Top with whipped cream.

Take the plunge at
Achievement Days!

Date:
Time:
Place:

See you there!

Achievement Days

Splish, Splash Water Fun and Safety

OUTDOOR FUN & SKILLS

GOAL #1:

Learn Water Safety Rules and Fun Water Activities

Learn water safety rules and fun water activities.

WATER SAFETY RULES: (1) Always swim with a friend. (2) Don't swim where it is too deep for your ability. (3) If the surf's up, wait until the water is safe; don't swim near ocean waves unless with an adult and you are an experienced swimmer. (4) Dive only into water where you know it is not shallow or rocky, clear of other swimmers. (5) Stay away from boats and water skiers. (6) Never swim in unfamiliar water; at first walk out and swim back in. (7) If using inflatable tubes, be careful not to drift out too far from shore. (8) If playing deep water games or when you're in a boat, always wear a fitted life jacket.

WATER FUN ACTIVITY IDEAS: ▫ Grapefruit Grab   ▫ Chug-a-Jug
   ▫ Water Tug of War   ▫ Water Ball Crisscross   ▫ Sink the Buoy
▫ Grasping for Straws   ▫ Bug Bite Tag   ▫ Soaked Shirt Relay

Splish Splash Water Fun Activities

GRAPEFRUIT GRAB: Play with two players or two teams. Start with 21 points. Toss a grapefruit back and forth across a dividing line (with markers on each side of the pool). Each time the grapefruit is passed, the player has five seconds to pass it back to the other side. Each time a player drops the grapefruit, she loses a point unless she can dive for it and bring it up before the person from the other team gets it.

CHUG-A-JUG: Players play in teams to chug (haul) a gallon plastic jug in each hand across the pool. You'll need four empty plastic gallon milk or punch jugs with the lid on (two for each team). Players line up in even teams. The first player for each team holds a jug in each hand. At "go" players race to the other side and back, swimming or floating. The moment they return, the other player on team starts. The first team to complete wins!

WATER TUG OF WAR: You'll need a long plastic rope. Place rope in the water and let it sink to the bottom. Have one person in the center as the center dividing line. Divide players into two teams standing on the sides of the pool. At "go" all players rush to their side of the rope, dive in and tug the rope. The winning team pulls the other team beyond the center dividing line. Rope for this game can also be used for the SWIM AND SINK THE BOUY game.

WATER BALL CRISSCROSS: You'll need two or four fabric water balls. Play with two players or two teams, divided standing in the pool 12 feet apart. At "go" the balls are thrown at the same time and balls are continually tossed to the other team, crossing each other, until one ball is not caught. Each time a ball is not caught, the other team earns a point. Teams play to 21 game points. This game is a lot of fun since it requires a lot of thought and coordination to keep the balls going back and forth at the same time. To keep the flow so that both teams throw their ball at the same time, you may want to have someone say "go" with each crisscross throw.

Splish Splash
Water Fun Activities

<u>GRAPEFRUIT GRAB</u>: Play with two players or two teams. Start with 21 points. Toss a grapefruit back and forth across a dividing line (with markers on each side of the pool). Each time the grapefruit is passed, the player has five seconds to pass it back to the other side. Each time a player drops the grapefruit, she loses a point unless she can dive for it and bring it up before the person from the other team gets it.

<u>CHUG-A-JUG</u>: Players play in teams to chug (haul) a gallon plastic jug in each hand across the pool. You'll need four empty plastic gallon milk or punch jugs with the lid on (two for each team). Players line up in even teams. The first player for each team holds a jug in each hand. At "go" players race to the other side and back, swimming or floating. The moment they return, the other player on team starts. The first team to complete wins!

<u>WATER TUG OF WAR</u>: <u>You'll need a long plastic rope</u>. Place rope in the water and let it sink to the bottom. Have one person in the center as the center dividing line. Divide players into two teams standing on the side of the pool. At "go" all players rush to their side of the rope, dive in and tug the rope. The winning team pulls the other team beyond the center dividing line. Rope for this game can also be used for the SWIM AND SINK THE BOUY game.

<u>WATER BALL CRISSCROSS</u>: <u>You'll need two or four fabric water balls</u>. Play with two players or two teams, divided standing in the pool 12 feet apart. At "go" the balls are thrown at the same time and balls are continually tossed to the other team, crossing each other, until one ball is not caught. Each time a ball is not caught, the other team earns a point. Teams play to 21 game points. This game is a lot of fun since it requires a lot of thought and coordination to keep the balls going back and forth at the same time. To keep the flow so that both teams throw their ball at the same time, you may want to have someone say "go" with each crisscross throw.

Splish Splash
Water Fun Activities

SINK THE BUOY: **You'll need four or more different colored mylar balloons** (that become the bouy) **and a rope or long piece of yarn.** Do not use laytex balloons in a pool; if a balloon pops, a child could swallow and choke on the pieces. Tie mylar balloons (buoys) 3 feet apart onto a long piece of yarn with another piece of yarn or string, stretching 15 or 20 feet across the pool. TO PLAY: Two players hold onto the yarn of balloons at each end, holding the balloons tight. Swimmers stand 6 feet away. Leader calls out "Sink the Buoy" and adds a color (for example, blue). Players race to push down the blue balloon, jumping over the yarn to get to the other side. The last player to sink the buoy (mylar balloon) has to stay on the other side. Repeat game until all players are out.

NOTE #1: Rope for this game can also be used for the WATER TUG OF WAR game. You'll need yarn or string to tie balloons onto the rope.

GRASPING FOR STRAWS: **You'll need a package of plastic straws.** Players divide into two teams, standing in the pool, forming a circle, five feet away from center. The leader tosses the straw into the center of the circle. Players rush to gather as many straws as they can. Teams bring their straws to the pool side and count them, recording their total. Play 5 or more times. The team with the highest number of straws wins!

BUG BITE TAG: Players play in a small shallow area, e.g., 8-10 feet square. A player is first chosen as It, and she tags another player by touching her. The area touched becomes the "bug bite." That player is now It, and must hold one hand on the "bug bite" while she tags the next person. Once It tags another player, she can let go of her "bug bite."

SOAKED SHIRT RELAY: Players divide in teams in a shallow pool. At "go" the first player in each team races to the other end, puts on the wet shirt, swims back to the head of the line, takes off shirt and hands it to the next player. Next player swims with shirt to the other end, puts it on and swims back. Repeat until last player on team completes race to win!

OUTDOOR FUN & SKILLS

Theme #2: Outdoor Cookout

LOCATION OF ACTIVITY: This activity can be an outing where you cook out in an open fire pit, or food can be cooked on a barbecue or at home in the oven.

<u>Invitation</u>: Copy-and-create invitation (page 74) to give girls a week before activity.

Icebreaker Activity: Learn to Build a Fire and Cook Outdoors

DO AHEAD: Go where you can build and cook over a fire with one or more of the recipe items. Or, cook these items on a backyard barbecue or indoor oven. Gather supplies.

SHOW HOW TO COOK CAMPFIRE FAVORITES USING AN OPEN FIRE, GRILL, or OVEN:

Follow the instructions below if building and cooking on a campfire, following the recipe(s) chosen from the Campfire Favorites recipes.

▪ <u>Choose Camp Site</u>: 1. Choose a location to build a fire 15 feet away from bushes, trees, or fallen trees, where there is plenty of kindling, tinder, and wood in the area to keep a healthy fire going.

▪ <u>Gather Kindling (2-6" pieces of wood), Tinder (dry grass/leaves), and Wood</u> to build the fire, storing wood 15 feet away from the fire circle.

▪ <u>Build a Fire Circle</u> by placing rocks around the fire area or dig a 2-foot pit in which to build a fire.

▪ <u>To Build a Small Crisscross Fire</u>: (1) Lay two 4" x 12" logs about 12 inches apart to create an air flow, or place three logs in an "A" frame. (2) Place tinder and kindling between the two logs or "A" frame logs.

(3) Place five small logs/twigs on top of log/frame and then layer five more on top crisscrossed, creating three layers. Roll up newspaper and place under the two logs next to the tinder and kindling, and light with a match or lighter. (4) To keep fire going, add more logs, keeping surface flat if you are cooking with Dutch ovens. You could even add barbecue coals to the fire in place of wood.

▪ <u>Put Out Fire</u> by breaking up fire with a stick and separating coals to cool. Sprinkle, don't pour water over coals to avoid steam burns.

<u>Caution</u>: Have a bucket of water and a shovel ready to put out the fire when needed. <u>Never</u> leave a fire unattended. Before leaving the campsite, make sure the fire is completely out and the ashes are buried before leaving it.

Goal #2 Activity: Learn to Cook Campfire Favorites recipes

YOU'LL NEED: Copy of goal card (page 74) and Campfire Favorites recipes (page 75) for each girl.

ACTIVITY (see goal card (page 74) for details.

Success Snack: Campfire Favorites

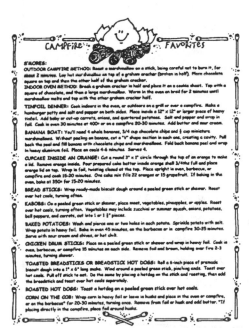

Have girls create foods from the Campfire Favorites recipes to share.

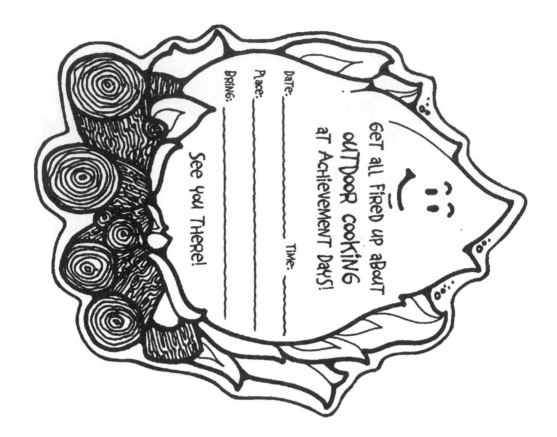

GeT all FiReD up aBouT
ouTDOOR CooKiNG
aT AchieveMeNT DaYS!

DaTe: _____

Place: _____   Time: _____

BRING: _____

See you THeRe!

Achievement Days

Outdoor Cookout

OUTDOOR FUN & SKILLS

GOAL #2:
Learn to Cook Campfire Favorite Recipes

Learn to cook one of the following Camping Favorite Recipes outside on a campfire, on a barbecue grill, or inside in the oven.

○ S'mores
○ Tinfoil Dinner
○ Banana Boat
○ Cupcake Inside an Orange
○ Bread Sticks
○ Kabobs
○ Baked Potatoes
○ Chicken Drum Sticks
○ Toasted Breadsticks or Breadstick Hotdogs
○ Roasted Hotdogs
○ Corn on the Cob

CAMPFIRE FAVORITES

S'MORES:
OUTDOOR CAMPFIRE METHOD: Roast a marshmallow on a stick, being careful not to burn it, for about 2 minutes. Lay hot marshmallow on top of a graham cracker (broken in half). Place chocolate square on top and then the other half of the graham cracker.
INDOOR OVEN METHOD: Break a graham cracker in half and place it on a cookie sheet. Top with a square of chocolate, and then a large marshmallow. Warm in the oven on broil for 2 minutes until marshmallow melts and top with the other graham cracker half.

TINFOIL DINNER: Cook indoors in the oven, or outdoors on a grill or over a campfire. Make a hamburger patty and salt and pepper on both sides. Place inside a 12" x 12" or larger piece of heavy tinfoil. Add baby or cut-up carrots, onions, and quartered potatoes. Salt and pepper and wrap in foil. Cook in oven 30 minutes at 400° or on a campfire 20-30 minutes. Add butter and sour cream.

BANANA BOAT: You'll need 4 whole bananas, 3/4 cup chocolate chips and ½ cup miniature marshmallows. Without peeling on banana, cut a "V" shape section in each one, creating a cavity. Pull back the peel and fill banana with chocolate chips and marshmallows. Fold back banana peel and wrap in heavy aluminum foil. Place on coals 4-6 minutes. Serves 4.

CUPCAKE INSIDE AN ORANGE: Cut a round 3" x 1" circle through the top of an orange to make a lid. Remove orange inside. Pour prepared cake batter inside orange shell 3/4ths full and place orange lid on top. Wrap in foil, twisting closed at the top. Place upright in oven, barbecue, or campfire and cook 15-20 minutes. One cake mix fills 22 oranges or 15 grapefruit. If baking in the oven, bake at 350° for 15-20 minutes.

BREAD STICKS: Wrap ready-made biscuit dough around a peeled green stick or skewer. Roast over hot coals, turning often.

KABOBS: On a peeled green stick or skewer, place meat, vegetables, pineapples, or apples. Roast over hot coals, turning often. Vegetables may include zucchini or summer squash, onions, potatoes, bell peppers, and carrots, cut into 1 or 1 ½" pieces.

BAKED POTATOES: Wash and pierce one or two holes in each potato. Sprinkle potato with salt. Wrap potato in heavy foil. Bake in oven 45 minutes, on the barbecue or in campfire 30-35 minutes. Serve with sour cream and chives, or hot chili.

CHICKEN DRUM STICKS: Place on a peeled green stick or skewer and wrap in heavy foil. Cook in oven, barbecue, or campfire 15 minutes on each side. Remove foil and brown, holding over fire 2-3 minutes, turning skewer.

TOASTED BREADSTICKS OR BREADSTICK HOT DOGS: Roll a 6-inch piece of premade biscuit dough into a 1" x 6" long snake. Wind around a peeled green stick, pinching ends. Toast over hot coals. Pull off stick to eat. Do the same by placing a hotdog on the stick and roasting, then add the breadstick and toast over hot coals separately.

ROASTED HOT DOGS: Toast a hotdog on a peeled green stick over hot coals.

CORN ON THE COB: Wrap corn in heavy foil or leave in husks and place in the oven or campfire, or on the barbecue* for 20-30 minutes, turning once. Remove from foil or husk and add butter. *If placing directly in the campfire, place foil around husks.

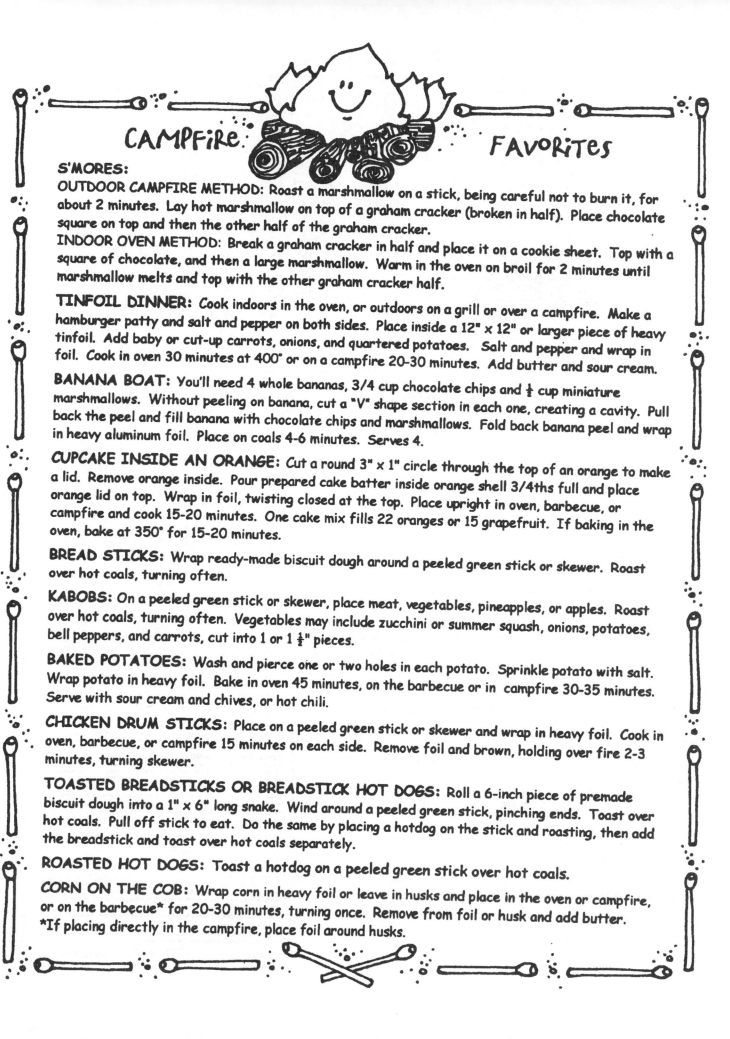

CAMPFIRE FAVORITES

S'MORES:

OUTDOOR CAMPFIRE METHOD: Roast a marshmallow on a stick, being careful not to burn it, for about 2 minutes. Lay hot marshmallow on top of a graham cracker (broken in half). Place chocolate square on top and then the other half of the graham cracker.

INDOOR OVEN METHOD: Break a graham cracker in half and place it on a cookie sheet. Top with a square of chocolate, and then a large marshmallow. Warm in the oven on broil for 2 minutes until marshmallow melts and top with the other graham cracker half.

TINFOIL DINNER: Cook indoors in the oven, or outdoors on a grill or over a campfire. Make a hamburger patty and salt and pepper on both sides. Place inside a 12" x 12" or larger piece of heavy tinfoil. Add baby or cut-up carrots, onions, and quartered potatoes. Salt and pepper and wrap in foil. Cook in oven 30 minutes at 400° or on a campfire 20-30 minutes. Add butter and sour cream.

BANANA BOAT: You'll need 4 whole bananas, 3/4 cup chocolate chips and ½ cup miniature marshmallows. Without peeling on banana, cut a "V" shape section in each one, creating a cavity. Pull back the peel and fill banana with chocolate chips and marshmallows. Fold back banana peel and wrap in heavy aluminum foil. Place on coals 4-6 minutes. Serves 4.

CUPCAKE INSIDE AN ORANGE: Cut a round 3" x 1" circle through the top of an orange to make a lid. Remove orange inside. Pour prepared cake batter inside orange shell 3/4ths full and place orange lid on top. Wrap in foil, twisting closed at the top. Place upright in oven, barbecue, or campfire and cook 15-20 minutes. One cake mix fills 22 oranges or 15 grapefruit. If baking in the oven, bake at 350° for 15-20 minutes.

BREAD STICKS: Wrap ready-made biscuit dough around a peeled green stick or skewer. Roast over hot coals, turning often.

KABOBS: On a peeled green stick or skewer, place meat, vegetables, pineapples, or apples. Roast over hot coals, turning often. Vegetables may include zucchini or summer squash, onions, potatoes, bell peppers, and carrots, cut into 1 or 1 ½" pieces.

BAKED POTATOES: Wash and pierce one or two holes in each potato. Sprinkle potato with salt. Wrap potato in heavy foil. Bake in oven 45 minutes, on the barbecue or in campfire 30-35 minutes. Serve with sour cream and chives, or hot chili.

CHICKEN DRUM STICKS: Place on a peeled green stick or skewer and wrap in heavy foil. Cook in oven, barbecue, or campfire 15 minutes on each side. Remove foil and brown, holding over fire 2-3 minutes, turning skewer.

TOASTED BREADSTICKS OR BREADSTICK HOT DOGS: Roll a 6-inch piece of premade biscuit dough into a 1" x 6" long snake. Wind around a peeled green stick, pinching ends. Toast over hot coals. Pull off stick to eat. Do the same by placing a hotdog on the stick and roasting, then add the breadstick and toast over hot coals separately.

ROASTED HOT DOGS: Toast a hotdog on a peeled green stick over hot coals.

CORN ON THE COB: Wrap corn in heavy foil or leave in husks and place in the oven or campfire, or on the barbecue* for 20-30 minutes, turning once. Remove from foil or husk and add butter.
*If placing directly in the campfire, place foil around husks.

PERSONAL PREPAREDNESS
Theme #1: Turn Over a New Leaf

<u>**Invitation:**</u> Copy-and-create invitation (page 77) to give girls a week before activity.

<u>Icebreaker Activity:</u>
<u>Turn Over a New Leaf</u>

DO AHEAD: Copy a set of eight New Leaf cards (page 78) on cardstock paper for each girl. Cut out cards, fold and glue each card back-to-back, and hide them around a room. Make a large sign that reads, "You can 'leaf' an old habit behind for a new."

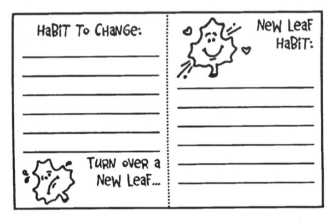

TURN OVER A NEW LEAF RACE:

1. As girls arrive, have them notice the new leaf cards around the room. Show one card with a bad habit written on one side and a new habit on the other. Discuss what it means to change a habit, to "turn over a new leaf," and how good they can feel with each bad habit they change.

2. Post sign and have them memorize: "You can 'leaf' an old habit behind for a new."

3. Gather leaves. Divide into two teams. At the word "go," each team races to find as many leaves as they can for their team (to win).

4. Place all of the cards in a center pile. At the word "go" each team races to grab one card at a time and turn it over so the "New Leaf Habit" side is facing up. Count cards to determine the winning team.

5. Tell girls, "We are all winners the moment we decide to 'turn over a new leaf' and change a habit. It all starts with a winning attitude."

<u>Goal #1 Activity: "Leaf" an Old Habit Behind for a New</u>

YOU'LL NEED: Copy of goal card (page 77) and two sets of New Leaf cards (page 78) for each girl, scissors, pencils, and markers.

ACTIVITY: See goal card (page 77) for details.

<u>Success Snack: Leaf Cookie</u>

Make round or square sugar cookies or leaf-shaped cookies and bake. Decorate a leaf on top with green or orange frosting. As they eat, tell girls it takes 15 seconds to change your attitude and "turn over a new leaf." Take the first five seconds to think about the habit they don't want. In the next five seconds have them imagine the desired habit. In the last five seconds, have girls "turn over the leaf" and begin their new habit.

TURN OVER a NEW Leaf
at Achievement Days!

Place: _____
Date: _____
Time: _____

See you there!

PERSONAL PREPAREDNESS

GOAL #1:

"Leaf" an Old Habit Behind for a New

Make a decision to change one or more habits using the New Leaf Habit card(s).

1. Write on one side the habit you want to change.
2. Then turn over a new leaf ... (turn the card over) and write the new leaf habit.

HaBiT To Change:	NEW LeaF HaBiT:
_____	_____
_____	_____
_____	_____
_____	_____
_____	_____
TURN oVer a NEW LeaF...	_____

YOU MAY WANT TO CHANGE THE WAY YOU DO THE FOLLOWING: groom, dress, clean your room, treat others, study in school, pay attention in class, greet friends, make friends, serve, do your chores, treat your parents or family, speak, take care of pets, organize your time, get to places on time, take care of your clothes, style your hair, etc.

EXAMPLE: One girl had a cluttered room and bathroom. To "turn over a new leaf" she posted a sign in each room with the number "3" on each. The signs reminded of her "new leaf" habit to "put 3 things away before she left each room." Because of this new habit, she felt better whenever she entered those rooms.

HaBiT To CHaNGe:

_____
_____
_____
_____

New LeaF
HaBiT:

_____
_____
_____
_____

TURN over a
New LeaF...

HaBiT To CHaNGe:

_____
_____
_____
_____

New LeaF
HaBiT:

_____
_____
_____
_____

TURN over a
New LeaF...

HaBiT To CHaNGe:

_____
_____
_____
_____

New LeaF
HaBiT:

_____
_____
_____
_____

TURN over a
New LeaF...

HaBiT To CHaNGe:

_____
_____
_____
_____

New LeaF
HaBiT:

_____
_____
_____
_____

TURN over a
New LeaF...

HaBiT To CHaNGe:

_____
_____
_____
_____

New LeaF
HaBiT:

_____
_____
_____
_____

TURN over a
New LeaF...

HaBiT To CHaNGe:

_____
_____
_____
_____

New LeaF
HaBiT:

_____
_____
_____
_____

TURN over a
New LeaF...

HaBiT To CHaNGe:

_____
_____
_____
_____

New LeaF
HaBiT:

_____
_____
_____
_____

TURN over a
New LeaF...

HaBiT To CHaNGe:

_____
_____
_____
_____

New LeaF
HaBiT:

_____
_____
_____
_____

TURN over a
New LeaF...

PERSONAL PREPAREDNESS

Theme #2: Bloom Where You're Planted

Invitation: Copy-and-create invitation (page 80) to give girls a week before activity.

Icebreaker Activity: Review the Have a Bloomin' Good Day! Poster

DO AHEAD: Copy the Have a Bloomin' Good Day! poster (page 81) for each girl. Supply pencils and markers.

REVIEW POSTER: Sitting at a table, give each girl poster and a pencil. Review the ideas on the poster and then brainstorm for more ideas on how girls can have a positive day. Have girls add their own ideas on the poster. Encourage them to post this in their room or on their mirror to review daily.

Goal #2 Activity: Schedule Your Goals to Blossom and Grow.

YOU'LL NEED: Copy of the goal card (page 80) and 12 Bloom Where Your Planted Calendar for each girl (page 82).

ACTIVITY: See goal card (page 80) for details.

Success Snack:

Bloom Where You're Planted Cupcakes.
Make and frost cupcakes and top with a frosted or cereal flower. You will find tiny flowers in a box of Trix (flower and fruit shaped) cereal. Tell girls that if they try to make the most out of each day, planning their time and using it wisely, they can bloom where they are planted. Ask them to look ahead and say, a year from now, where do I want to be? Will I get there if I am doing what I am doing today? The time is going to go by anyway, so you might as well "bloom!" Make progress towards your goal each day.

Come to
Achievement Days!

Date: _____ Time: _____

Place: _____

See you there!

Do you want to blossom and grow?

Achievement Days

Bloom Where You're Planted

PERSONAL PREPAREDNESS

GOAL #2:

Schedule Your Goals to Blossom and Grow

Have a Bloomin' Good Day!

Appreciate what you have.

Don't forget to pray.

Wake up happy.

Plan your day.

Focus on others instead of yourself.

Make the best of every situation.

Don't procrastinate a problem.

Add your own ideas on how you could have a positive day!

1. Study the Bloom Where You're Planted poster to learn ways you can make each day a positive day. Add your own ideas on how you can have a positive day! Then post them on the wall as a reminder.

2. Write your goals on the Bloom Where You're Planted! calendar each month. Then watch yourself grow as you achieve each goal. Divide goals into daily steps.

BLOOM where you're planted!

Month _____ Year _____

Sunday	Monday	Tuesday	Wednesday	Thursday	Friday	Saturday
○	○	○	○	○	○	○
○	○	○	○	○	○	○
○	○	○	○	○	○	○
○	○	○	○	○	○	○
○	○	○	○	○	○	○

BLOOM

_____
Month

Year

where you're planted!

Sunday	Monday	Tuesday	Wednesday	Thursday	Friday	Saturday
○	○	○	○	○	○	○
○	○	○	○	○	○	○
○	○	○	○	○	○	○
○	○	○	○	○	○	○
○	○	○	○	○	○	○

SAFETY & EMERGENCY PREPAREDNESS

Theme #1: Ladybug Fire Safety

Invitation: Copy-and-create invitation (page 85) to give girls a week before activity. Color and cut out invitation. Glue part A over B at the top, fold and open.

Icebreaker Activity: Ladybug Fire Drill Game

GATHER SUPPLIES: Four ping-pong balls, red and black permanent markers, a straw for each girl, blueprint of a home or house plan drawn on paper approximately blueprint size, firetraps (page 86), 8-10 small paper cups, scissors, and tape.

TO MAKE GAME:

1. With a black and red marker draw a ladybug on four different ping-pong balls, writing a number 1, 2, 3, or 4 on each ball.

2. Mount the blueprint or drawn house plan on the table, taping down the edges so the plan lays flat against the tabletop.

3. Cut off the rolled edge on one side of each paper cup. Tape the cut side of each cup onto the table by each window and door exit, so the ball can roll over the exit smoothly into the cup.

4. Color and cut out the firetraps and place double-stick tape on the back ready to mount on the house plan.

INTRODUCE FIRE SAFETY:

1. Tell girls the poem "Ladybug, ladybug, fly away home ... your house is on fire and your children alone."

2. Talk about fire safety and developing a fire escape route for your family. This is especially important if the girls are alone or when they are caring for children.

3. Tell them that after they play the game, they will learn the Ladybug Fire Escape Rules (page 87).

TO PLAY THE LADYBUG FIRE DRILL GAME:

1. Have four girls at a time choose a ladybug ping pong ball and remember the number written on their ball (1, 2, 3, or 4) in case they get mixed up while playing. 2. Have them choose a location in the home and place their ladybug ball in that room.

3. Now, place the firetraps at various spots in the house with some blocking a window or access down a hall, or wherever you wish to place them.

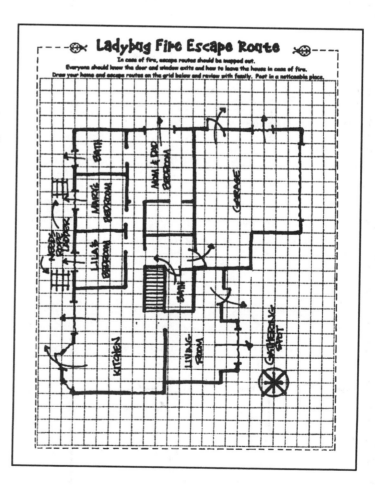

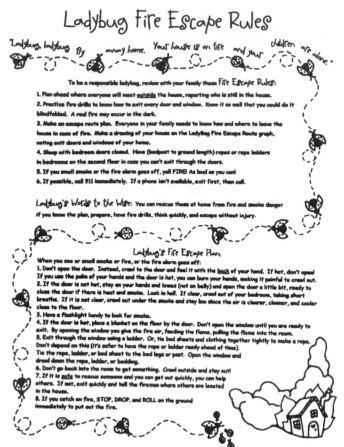

Ladybug Fire Escape Rules

Ladybug, ladybug fly away home. Your house is on fire and your children are alone.

To be a responsible ladybug, review with your family these Fire Escape Rules:

1. Plan ahead where everyone will meet <u>outside</u> the house, reporting who is still in the house.
2. Practice fire drills to know how to exit every door and window. Know it so well that you could do it blindfolded. A real fire may occur in the dark.
3. Make an escape route plan. Everyone in your family needs to know how and where to leave the house in case of fire. Make a drawing of your house on the LadyBug Fire Escape Route graph, noting exit doors and windows of your home.
4. Sleep with bedroom doors closed. Have (bedpost to ground length) ropes or rope ladders in bedrooms on the second floor in case you can't exit through the doors.
5. If you smell smoke or the fire alarm goes off, yell FIRE! As loud as you can!
6. If possible, call 911 immediately. If a phone isn't available, exit first, then call.

Ladybug's Words to the Wise: You can rescue those at home from fire and smoke danger if you know the plan, prepare, have fire drills, think quickly, and escape without injury.

Ladybug's Fire Escape Plan:

When you see or smell smoke or fire, or the fire alarm goes off:
1. Don't open the door. Instead, crawl to the door and feel it with the <u>back</u> of your hand. If hot, don't open! If you use the palm of your hands and the door is hot, you can burn your hands, making it painful to crawl out.
2. If the door is not hot, stay on your hands and knees (not on belly) and open the door a little bit, ready to close the door if there is heat and smoke. Look in hall. If clear, crawl out of your bedroom, taking short breaths. If it is not clear, crawl out under the smoke and stay low since the air is clearer, cleaner, and cooler close to the floor.
3. Have a flashlight handy to look for smoke.
4. If the door is hot, place a blanket on the floor by the door. Don't open the window until you are ready to exit. By opening the window you give the fire air, feeding the flame, pulling the flame into the room.
5. Exit through the window using a ladder. Or, tie bed sheets and clothing together tightly to make a rope. Don't depend on this (it's safer to have the rope or ladder ready ahead of time). Tie the rope, ladder, or bed sheet to the bed legs or post. Open the window and crawl down the rope, ladder, or bedding.
6. Don't go back into the room to get something. Crawl outside and stay out!
7. If it is <u>safe</u> to rescue someone and you can get out quickly, you can help others. If not, exit quickly and tell the fireman where others are located in the house.
8. If you catch on fire, STOP, DROP, and ROLL on the ground immediately to put out the fire.

3. At the word "go" each girl, using a straw, will blow her ladybug ball, trying to get out of the house, trying to avoid the firetraps, finding an exit, and blowing her ball out the exit into a paper cup.

RULES:

4. Players must not go through any walls or firetraps. If they blow the ladybug ball through a wall or accidently cross a firetrap, they must start again from their original position.
5. You may want to award the first one to escape with a hot tamale or red-hot candy treat!
6. Once all the girls have escaped safely from the home, let the next four girls play. You will need to remove the firetraps from the house plan. Allow the new girls to find position their ladybug. Then, place the firetraps in different places than in the previous game.

REVIEW:

7. Have girls talk about their safe escape or the difficulties they encountered while escaping.

GOAL #1 ACTIVITY: Learn How to Escape from a Fire

YOU'LL NEED: Copy of the goal card (page 84), Ladybug Fire Escape Rules and three Ladybug Fire Escape Route (pages 87-88) for each girl.

ACTIVITY:

1. Review the Ladybug Fire Escape Rules and anticipate moves, looking at the house plan on the table.
2. Have girls take the Ladybug Fire Escape Route home and draw their house plan with the window and door exits. See goal card (page 85) for details.
3. Girls could take three Lady Bug Fire Escape Route pages if they have three floors in their home (one for each floor).

Success Snack: Ladybug Cool Off Lemonade

1. Make the ladybug straw decoration (page 89) for each girl, serve lemonade and attach decoration to the straw (punching holes first).
2. Talk about ways you can stay cool in a fire (see Escape Rules).
3. Tell girls that a fire can spread through your house in minutes and can become as hot as 600° F.

> **COOL WAYS:**
> 1. Crawl.
> 2. STOP, DROP, and ROLL if on fire.
> 3. Follow rules.

A

Ladybug,

Ladybug...

B

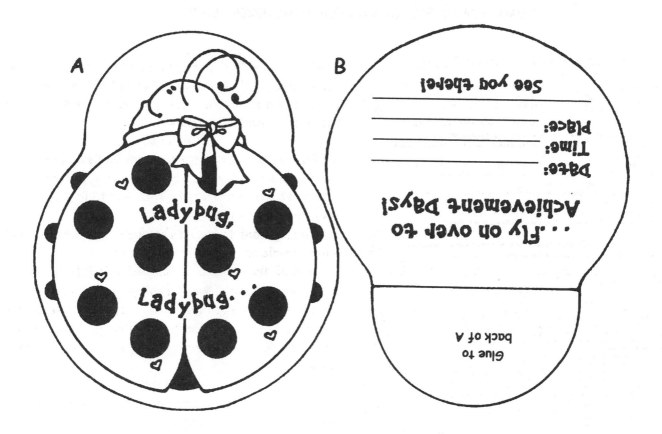

Achievement Days

Ladybug, Ladybug Fly Away Home FIRE SAFETY

SAFETY & EMERGENCY PREPAREDNESS

Ladybug Fire Escape Rules

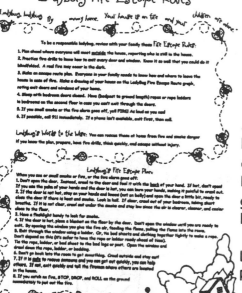

Ladybug, ladybug fly away home. Your house is on fire and your children are alone.

To be a responsible ladybug, review with your family these Fire Escape Rules:

1. Plan ahead where everyone will meet outside the house, reporting who is still in the house.
2. Practice fire drills to know how to exit every door and window. Know it so well that you could do it blindfolded. A real fire may occur in the dark.
3. Make an escape route plan. Everyone in your family needs to know how and where to leave the house in case of fire. Make a drawing of your house on the Ladybug Fire Escape Route graph, noting exit doors and windows of your home.
4. Sleep with bedroom doors closed. Have (buoyant to ground length) ropes or rope ladders in bedrooms on the second floor in case you can't exit through the doors.
5. If you smell smoke or the fire alarm goes off, yell FIRE! As loud as you can!
6. If possible, call 911 immediately. If a phone isn't available, exit first, then call.

Ladybug's Words to the Wise: You can rescue those at home from fire and smoke danger if you know the plan, prepare, have fire drills, think quickly, and escape without injury.

Ladybug's Fire Escape Plan

When you see or small smoke or fire, or the fire alarm goes off:
1. Don't open the door. Instead, crawl to the door and feel it with the back of your hand. If hot, don't open!
2. If you use the palm of your hands and the door is hot, you can burn your hands, making it painful to crawl out.
3. If the door is not hot, stay on your hands and knees (not on belly) and open the door a little bit, ready to close the door if there is heat and smoke. Look in hall. If clear, crawl out of your bedroom, taking short breaths. If it is not clear, crawl and under the smoke and stay since the air is clearer, cleaner, and cooler close to the floor.
4. If the door is hot, place a blanket on the floor by the door. Don't open the window until you are ready to exit. By opening the window you give the fire air, feeding the flame, pulling the flame into the room.
5. Exit through the window using a ladder. Or, tie bed sheets and clothing together tightly to make a rope. Don't depend on this (It's safer to have the rope or ladder ready ahead of time.) Tie the rope, ladder or bed sheet to the bed legs or post. Open the window and crawl down the rope, ladder, or bedding.
6. Don't go back into the room to get something. Crawl outside and stay out!
7. If it is safe to rescue someone and you can get out quickly, you can help others. If not, exit quickly and tell the firemen where others are located in the house.
8. If you catch on fire, STOP, DROP, and ROLL on the ground immediately to put out the fire.

GOAL #1:
Learn How to Escape from a Fire

Make a fire escape plan of your home with your family and have a fire drill. You can use the Ladybug Fire Escape Route graph paper to map out your home windows and door exits.

Learn the Ladybug Fire Escape Rules.

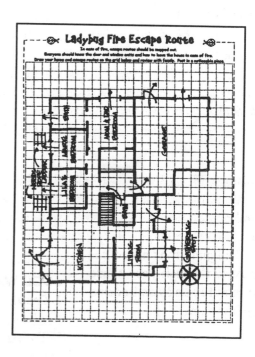

Ladybug Fire Escape Rules

"Ladybug, ladybug fly away home. Your house is on fire and your children are alone."

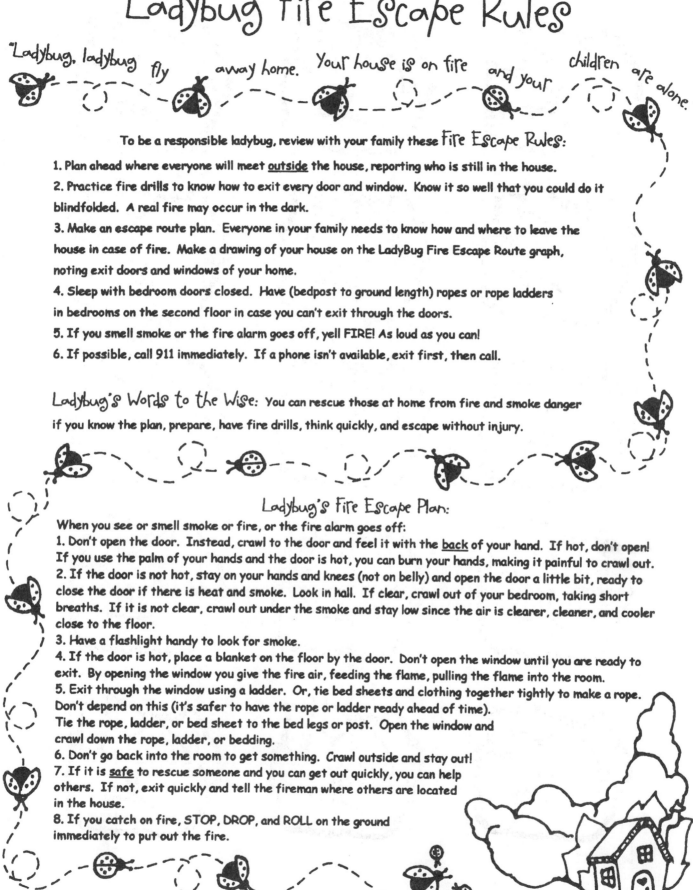

To be a responsible ladybug, review with your family these Fire Escape Rules:

1. Plan ahead where everyone will meet <u>outside</u> the house, reporting who is still in the house.

2. Practice fire drills to know how to exit every door and window. Know it so well that you could do it blindfolded. A real fire may occur in the dark.

3. Make an escape route plan. Everyone in your family needs to know how and where to leave the house in case of fire. Make a drawing of your house on the LadyBug Fire Escape Route graph, noting exit doors and windows of your home.

4. Sleep with bedroom doors closed. Have (bedpost to ground length) ropes or rope ladders in bedrooms on the second floor in case you can't exit through the doors.

5. If you smell smoke or the fire alarm goes off, yell FIRE! As loud as you can!

6. If possible, call 911 immediately. If a phone isn't available, exit first, then call.

Ladybug's Words to the Wise: You can rescue those at home from fire and smoke danger if you know the plan, prepare, have fire drills, think quickly, and escape without injury.

Ladybug's Fire Escape Plan:

When you see or smell smoke or fire, or the fire alarm goes off:

1. Don't open the door. Instead, crawl to the door and feel it with the <u>back</u> of your hand. If hot, don't open! If you use the palm of your hands and the door is hot, you can burn your hands, making it painful to crawl out.

2. If the door is not hot, stay on your hands and knees (not on belly) and open the door a little bit, ready to close the door if there is heat and smoke. Look in hall. If clear, crawl out of your bedroom, taking short breaths. If it is not clear, crawl out under the smoke and stay low since the air is clearer, cleaner, and cooler close to the floor.

3. Have a flashlight handy to look for smoke.

4. If the door is hot, place a blanket on the floor by the door. Don't open the window until you are ready to exit. By opening the window you give the fire air, feeding the flame, pulling the flame into the room.

5. Exit through the window using a ladder. Or, tie bed sheets and clothing together tightly to make a rope. Don't depend on this (it's safer to have the rope or ladder ready ahead of time). Tie the rope, ladder, or bed sheet to the bed legs or post. Open the window and crawl down the rope, ladder, or bedding.

6. Don't go back into the room to get something. Crawl outside and stay out!

7. If it is <u>safe</u> to rescue someone and you can get out quickly, you can help others. If not, exit quickly and tell the fireman where others are located in the house.

8. If you catch on fire, STOP, DROP, and ROLL on the ground immediately to put out the fire.

Ladybug Fire Escape Route

In case of fire, escape routes should be mapped out.
Everyone should know the door and window exits and how to leave the house in case of fire.
Draw your home and escape routes on the grid below and review with family. Post in a noticeable place.

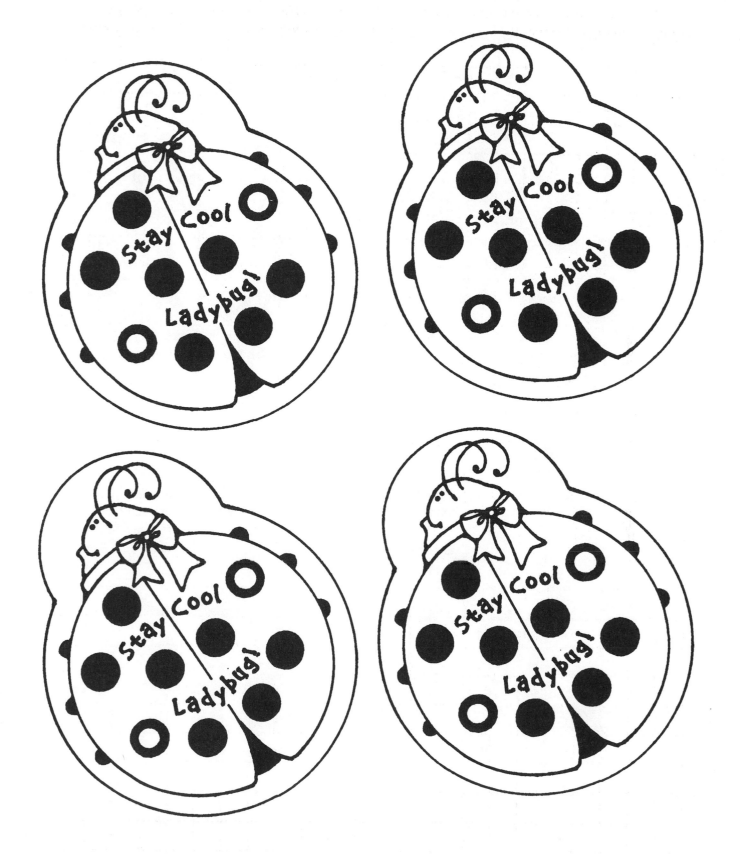

SAFETY & EMERGENCY PREPAREDNESS

Theme #2: Stranger Danger

Invitation: Copy-and-create invitation (page 91) to give girls a week before activity. Fold the invitation twice so Stranger Danger! Sign is in front.

Theme #2: Stranger Danger **Icebreaker Activity:** **Talk About Stranger Danger**

Strangers don't always look scary. But what do you do when you see or feel uncomfortable or are threatened by a stranger? Story: A woman was in her front yard with two children when a man drove up and said he was lost. The woman felt she and the children were in danger, but she always wanted to be nice to others. Not wanting to offend the man, she walked up to him to give directions. He grabbed her and tried to take her away in his car. She managed to get away from him and ran into the house, taking her children with her. What could she have done in this situation to say "no" to this stranger?

Goal #2 Activity: Learn Stranger Dangers and How to Stay Safe

YOU'LL NEED: Copy of the goal card (page 91) and the Stranger Danger cards and clue words (pages 92-96) for each girl. Cut out cards and clues and place in a zip-close bag for each girl.
ACTIVITY: Play the Stranger Danger Game to learn how to be safe at home and away from home. See goal card (page 91) for game details.

Success Snack: Danger Clue Cupcakes. Tell girls that some of the cupcakes have a clue inside that will "clue" them into a safety rule they must always remember.
TO MAKE:
1. Bake 9 or more cupcakes*.
2. Copy the 10 words/wordstrips (page 96) that read: (1) BE (2) AWARE (3) IT'S (4) BETTER (5) TO (6) BE (7) SAFE (8) THAN (9) SORRY. (10) SORRY NO CLUE.
3. Stuff a wordstrip in each cupcake by folding wordstrip and wrapping in tinfoil. Then insert a knife into the cupcake and slip the foil-covered wordstrip inside.
4. Frost and serve.

*If there are more than 9 girls, add a SORRY NO CLUE wordstrip in each additional cupcake. The 9 cupcakes must be eaten to retrieve all the messages. To keep track of these, place a toothpick in each until served. If you have less than 10 girls, place two wordstrips inside cupcakes.
   MESSAGE IS: BE AWARE ... IT'S BETTER TO BE SAFE THAN SORRY.

Fold

Fold

Come to Achievement Days and learn how to keep safe!

Date: _____

Time: _____

Place: _____

See you there!

STRANGER DANGER!

Achievement Days

Stranger Danger

SAFETY & EMERGENCY PREPAREDNESS

GOAL #2: Learn About Stranger Dangers and How to Be Safe

Play the Stranger Danger Game to learn how to be safe at home and away from home. This game can be shared with your family.

STRANGER DANGER GAME:

TO MAKE GAME: Cut out the Stranger Danger cards and place them in the center with players sitting in a circle on the floor. Place the missing words/clues face up in the center. Place the Stranger Danger cards in a stack. Take turns choosing a Stranger Danger card and reading it aloud. Search for the missing word/clue on the floor to fill in the blank. If player cannot find the answer or missing word, choose a safety buddy to help them find the answer. Read the question and answer aloud to review.

TO REVIEW: Divide into two teams, splitting cards equally among the teams. Teams take turns reading and completing cards aloud, without the words/clues. Read the questions as a team and try to complete the questions as a team, filling in the blanks. The team that completes the most cards wins.

STRANGER DANGER
Question #3: If you suspect
there is a stranger in
and you are near
to?

STRANGER DANGER
Question #1: How do you know
a person is a stranger?
ANSWER: Someone you don't
know or
_____ _____ _____

Stranger Danger cards

STRANGER DANGER

Question #1: How do you know a person is a stranger?

ANSWER: Someone you don't know or __ __ __ __ __.

STRANGER DANGER
Question #5: If a stranger tries to touch you or force you to go with him/her, what should you do?
ANSWER: Run away and scream for help. If you can't run away, act like a kitten that doesn't like to be picked up. You should __ __ __ __ and scratch.

STRANGER DANGER
Question #2: How would you prepare and what would you do if a stranger came into your home?
ANSWER: Before this could ever happen, record important __ __ __ __ __ numbers of nearby neighbors and the police on cards and place in rooms where you could grab the phone, lock the door, and call the police.

STRANGER DANGER
Question #6: When it gets dark and you are trying to stay safe in your house, what should you do?
ANSWER: Don't wait until it's dark to do something. When it starts to get dark, turn on the porch lights and close the __ __ __ __ __ __.

STRANGER DANGER
Question #3: If you suspect that there is a stranger in your home and you are near an exit, what do you do?
ANSWER: Go __ __ __ of your home to a neighbor's and call the police.

STRANGER DANGER
Question #7: How do you know when you are in a scary situation?
ANSWER: Trust your instincts. If a situation feels uncomfortable or scary, get __ __ __ __ as fast as you can.

STRANGER DANGER:
Question #4: If a call comes from a stranger and an adult is not at home, what do you say?
ANSWER: "He/she can't come to the phone right now. I can take a message." If the stranger keeps asking questions, __ __ __ __ up the phone.

STRANGER DANGER
Question #8: What should you do when you try to enter your home and the door is unlocked and/or a window has been broken?
ANSWER: Don't __ __ __ __ __ the home unless you have an adult or policeman with you to investigate.

STRANGER DANGER

<u>Question #9</u>: Why is an unlocked door or window an invitation to a stranger?

ANSWER: They make for an easy __ __ __ __ __ into your home.

STRANGER DANGER

<u>Question #13</u>: Shouldn't you be nice to everyone, even a stranger?

ANSWER: Never be afraid of offending someone you don't know. You don't __ __ __ a stranger anything, not even a hello.

STRANGER DANGER

<u>Question #10</u>: Should you answer the door when you are the only one home ?

ANSWER: If a stranger knocks when you are home __ __ __ __ __, ask him to come back later.

STRANGER DANGER

<u>Question #14</u>: If a policeman tries to enter you home when you have not called him/her, what should you do?

ANSWER: Ask through the window or bolted door what they want and ask to see their identification and __ __ __ __ __ before you let them in.

STRANGER DANGER

<u>Question #11</u>: If you must walk home alone and you are away from your neighborhood, what should you do?

ANSWER: Insist on someone going with you to call a friend to __ __ __ __ __ you up. Keep emergency phone numbers for friends and neighbors with you at all times.

STRANGER DANGER

<u>Question #15</u>: If someone follows you in their car, what do you do?

ANSWER: Go to the nearest McGruff House or __ __ __ __ house. Don't walk outside your neighborhood alone. Always have a friend.

STRANGER DANGER

<u>Question #12</u>: Should you give your phone number to everyone who asks for it?

ANSWER: Say __ __ when a stranger asks for your phone number.

STRANGER DANGER

<u>Question #16</u>: If you are lost, what do you do?

ANSWER: Ask a woman to __ __ __ __ you rather than asking a strange man to help.

STRANGER DANGER

<u>Question #17</u>: What are the rules for safety when you go to a stranger's house selling things?

ANSWER: Have someone with you and never ___ ___ ___ ___ ___ ___ an invitation to go inside their house.

STRANGER DANGER

<u>Question #21</u>: If someone other than your usual ride comes to pick you up from school, a lesson, or an event, how do you know if you should ride home with them?

ANSWER: You and your parents alone invent secret ___ ___ ___ ___ word(s), e.g., "crackers and pickles" that the person picking you up must say. Change code often.

STRANGER DANGER

<u>Question #18</u>: What does Check Point Charlie mean?

ANSWER: This means you tell someone where you are going and when you will be there. Then ___ ___ ___ ___ when you arrive.

STRANGER DANGER

<u>Question #22</u>: What if a stranger stops me on the street and asks me a question? Shouldn't I try to help them?

ANSWER: You don't need to answer a stranger's questions. Don't go ___ ___ ___ ___ them or the car or they could pull you in.

STRANGER DANGER

<u>Question #19</u>: When it's time to get into your own car, how do you know a stranger won't be there waiting for you?

ANSWER: ___ ___ ___ ___ inside your car and check front and back seats and trunk area. Always lock car before leaving. Lock the door as soon as you are in the car.

STRANGER DANGER

<u>Question #23</u>: When walking to a friend's house, how can you get there safely?

ANSWER: Call her the minute you leave and have her ___ ___ ___ ___ you halfway (if she is in the same neighborhood).

STRANGER DANGER

<u>Question #20</u>: If a stranger asks you to help them find their cat or dog, do you help them?

ANSWER: Don't get ___ ___ ___ ___ ___ to strangers or get talked into helping a stranger look for a pet or any other person, place, or thing.

STRANGER DANGER

<u>Question #24</u>: What about when I babysit away from home?

ANSWER: Have the children's ___ ___ ___ ___ ___ ___ pick you up and take you home, rather than the children's father.

STRANGER DANGER

Question #25: If a behavior is not appropriate, even with family members, what should you do?
ANSWER:

___ ___ ___ ___ ___ ___ it to another adult or parent, even if you're told not to tell anyone.

STRANGER DANGER

Question #29: How do I know if a home is a safe place to babysit?
ANSWER: Only babysit where your parents ___ ___ ___ ___ the family you are tending for.

STRANGER DANGER

Question #26: What does it mean that there is safety in numbers? ANSWER: Walk to school or to a friend's house with someone. Even in your own neighborhood you need someone to walk with you or ___ ___ ___ ___ until you have arrived safely.

STRANGER DANGER

Question #30: Is it necessary to know when your parents or those you are babysitting for return home? ANSWER: Yes, because when the garage or door opens you will know it's them. Always let parents open the door with their own ___ ___ ___. Don't open the door.

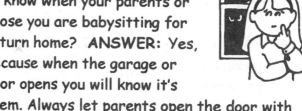

STRANGER DANGER

Question #27: Who do I call when I am alone or babysitting if I suspect a stranger is near?
ANSWER: Always have a ___ ___ ___ ___ of emergency phone numbers and nearby neighbors for your home and the place where you are tending.

STRANGER DANGER

Question #31: When you are at a friend's house or babysitting how will the police know where to find you if you call?
ANSWER: Always ___ ___ ___ ___ ___ down the name, address, and phone number of the place you are tending in case you have to call the police or your parents for help.

STRANGER DANGER

Question # 28: What if I want to visit a friend or neighbor?
ANSWER: Let your parents know where you are at all times or when you go from one friend's house to the next. Tell them your ___ ___ ___ ___ ___ ___ ___ ___.

STRANGER DANGER

Question #32: What do you say when you're babysitting or alone and a stranger calls?
ANSWER: Never say that you are the babysitter or that you are alone. Tell them that the person they are asking for is ___ ___ ___ ___, and he or she can't come to the phone. Ask who is calling and write down the name and phone number.

STRANGER DANGER

<u>Question #33</u>: What if I am taken away by a stranger and can't find my way home?

ANSWER: Look at signs and

_ _ _ _ _ _ _ _ _

to identify where you can be found if you can get to a phone. Always carry change in case you need it to make a phone call.

STRANGER DANGER GAME: See rules on the Stranger Danger Goal #1 instruction card.

STRANGER DANGER CLUES (answers): #1 trust #2 phone #3 out #4 hang #5 bite #6 blinds #7 away #8 enter #9 entry #10 alone #11 pick #12 no #13 owe #14 badge #15 safe #16 help #17 accept #18 call #19 look #20 close #21 code #22 near #23 meet #24 mother #25 report #26 watch #27 list #28 location #29 know #30 key #31 write #32 busy #33 addresses

DANGER CLUE CUPCAKE wordstrips:

BE	AWARE ...	IT'S	BETTER	TO
BE	SAFE	THAN	SORRY.	SORRY NO CLUE
SORRY NO CLUE	SORRY NO CLUE	SORRY NO CLUE	SORRY NO CLUE	
SORRY NO CLUE	SORRY NO CLUE	SORRY NO CLUE	SORRY NO CLUE	
SORRY NO CLUE	SORRY NO CLUE	SORRY NO CLUE	SORRY NO CLUE	
SORRY NO CLUE	SORRY NO CLUE	SORRY NO CLUE	SORRY NO CLUE	

STRANGER DANGER clue/answers:

trust   phone

out   hang   bite   blinds

away   enter   entry   alone

pick   no   owe   badge

safe   help   accept   call

look   close   code   near

meet   mother   report   watch

list   location   know   key

write   busy   addresses

SERVICE & CITIZENSHIP

Theme #1: Scatter Sunshine Senior Service

NOTE: This should be done in two activities. The first week do the Ice-breaker Activities below, preparing to visit seniors; the second week make your visit.

Invitation: Copy-and-create invitation (page 98) to give girls a week before activity. You may want to make two invitations (one for the first week and one for the second week; see above).

Icebreaker Activities:

Prepare for Your Senior Sunshine Visit

DO THE FOLLOWING BEFORE YOU VISIT SENIORS:

1. PRACTICE SKIT OR TALENT SHOW to entertain seniors, trying to involve seniors as you perform.

2. GATHER SUPPLIES FOR YOUR VISIT: See goal card for ideas.

3. SING the hymn "Scatter Sunshine." Invite seniors to join in the chorus, singing, "Scatter sunshine all along your way. Cheer and bless and brighten every passing day." See *Hymns*, page 230, "Scatter Sunshine."

4. SHARE SENIOR VISIT IDEAS: Talk about ways you could cheer and bless and brighten a senior's day. Tell girls that each senior has individual needs, likes and dislikes, hobbies and things they like to do. It takes a few visits before you know how they will react to various activities.

5. SHARE THE REWARDS FOR SENIOR SERVICE: Friendship, gratitude, wisdom, empathy, desire to serve, a sense of feeling needed, opportunity to develop listening skills and use talents, learn about others' experiences, share own thoughts and feelings, feel joy and satisfaction.

6. REVIEW "MY SUNSHINE FRIEND SPOTLIGHT" so that you will feel comfortable asking questions to seniors. Copy one or two Spotlights (page 99) for each girl. A copy of the finished My Sunshine Friend Spotlight could be sent with the thank-you card (see #8).

7. BRING CAMERAS to the senior visit so that photos can be taken of girls with their senior friends. Photos could also be placed inside the thank-you card (see #8).

8. PREPARE A THANK-YOU CARD that girls can send to the seniors after their visit. Copy "Thanks for sharing your sunshine" card (page 100) for each girl.

Goal #1 Activity: Interview and Enjoy Fun Activities with the Elderly.

YOU'LL NEED: Copy of the goal card and My Sunshine Friend Spotlight (pages 98-100) for each girl.
ACTIVITY: Choose from the activity ideas on the goal card (page 98).

Success Snack: Sunny Snacks.

Girls can make and take these sunny snacks to their senior friends and enjoy (be aware of special diets): ✿ Cheerful cupcakes or cookies: Frost and add a smile face with candies. ✿ Give them Goldfish crackers with smiles on them.

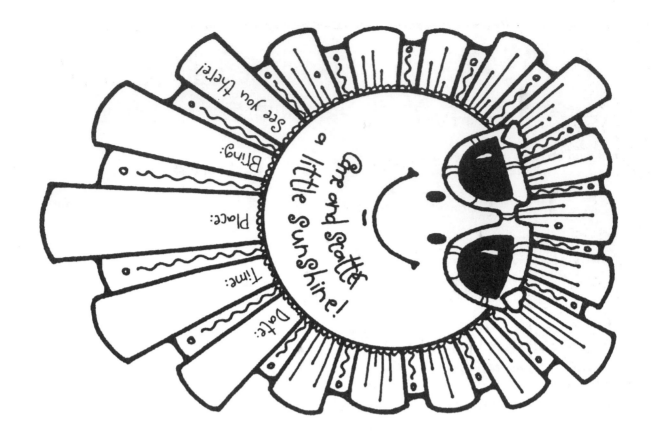

Inside the sun illustration:
Come and scatter a little sunshine!

Date:
Time:
Place:
Bring:
See you there!

Achievement Days

Scatter Sunshine: Senior Service

SERVICE & CITIZENSHIP

GOAL #1: Enjoy Fun Activities with the Elderly

Visit and enjoy fun activities with seniors. IDEAS:

☼ **SENIOR SKITS OR TALENT SHOW:** Make up skits or a talent show ahead of time to perform for senior friends. Subjects: Fairy tales, acting out a favorite children's story, an old movie, or their own version of fun.

☼ **MY SUNSHINE FRIEND SPOTLIGHT:** Take one or two My Sunshine Friend Spotlight forms and interview seniors, writing down things you learn about them.

☼ **SENIOR MAKE-OVER:** Bring supplies to do the nails and hair of those who want a make-over.

☼ **SUNSHINE THANK-YOU CARD:** After your visit, send a Thanks for Sharing Your Sunshine card. While you are there, if you take a picture of you and the senior together, this could be included in the card.

☼ **PLAY GAMES:** Bring games to play with seniors, e.g., Skip-bo, checkers, Pass the Pig, bingo, Pictionary, Taboo, Chinese Checkers, Guesstures, Clue, or others.

☼ **SEND A THANK-YOU CARD.**

My Sunshine Friend Spotlight

Your Name:

Age: Birthday: Phone #:

Address:

Where have you lived?

What do you love most about your family?

How big is your family?

If married, how did you meet your spouse?

What one thing have you accomplished in your life?

What do you like to do the most?

What is your funniest experience?

What games do you like?

What is your favorite food?

My Sunshine Friend Spotlight

Your Name:

Age: Birthday: Phone #:

Address:

Where have you lived?

What do you love most about your family?

How big is your family?

If married, how did you meet your spouse?

What one thing have you accomplished in your life?

What do you like to do the most?

What is your funniest experience?

What games do you like?

What is your favorite food?

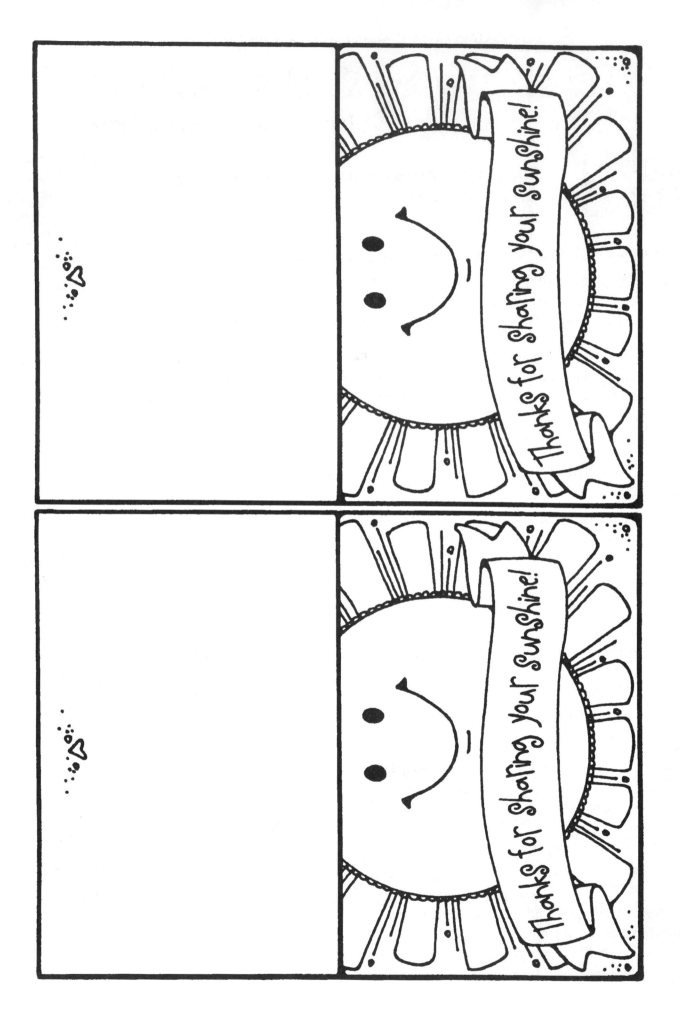

SERVICE & CITIZENSHIP

Theme #2: Entertain Children While Parents Serve

Invitation: Copy-and-create invitation (page 101) to give girls a week before activity.

Icebreaker Activity: Practice Games and Activities for Teddy Bear Party or Party of Your Choice

DO AHEAD: Gather supplies the Teddy Bear Party games and activities. See party plan (pages 103-107). Copy a set of stickers, have a sample paper plate, cup, and lunch sack to show how to decorate these for the party.

ACTIVITY: Have a practice session for the Teddy Bear Party so girls can put on a party for the children in the ward while their parents serve. Review how the stickers can be used in three ways: (1) prizes for games, (2) decorations for paper plate and cup, (3) decorations for the Teddy Bear Snack Sack.

GOAL MOTIVATION ACTIVITY — Goal #2: Put on a Party to Entertain Children While Parents Serve

ACTIVITY:

1. Arrange ahead of time a special day or night when girls can entertain children in the ward while parents serve (such as temple night, adult ward party, Relief Society Enrichment meeting, Young Women New Beginnings program, or a special community cleanup or other volunteer program).

2. When the date for the party has been scheduled, assign girls different tasks for the Teddy Bear Party (pages 103-1007) or another party of their choice.

PARTY PLAN IDEAS: See the goal card (page 102) and Teddy Bear's Party plan (pages 103-107) for details.

Success Snack: Teddy Bear Party Snacks/Food. Choose from all or some of the treat and food ideas in the Teddy Bear Party to show girls how to give out snacks children can win and put in their Teddy Bear Snack Sack, and food they can serve on the decorated plates and cups.

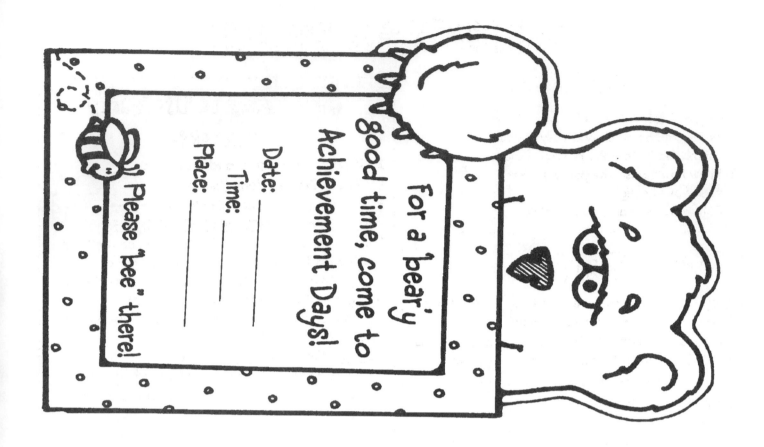

For a 'bear'y
good time, come to
Achievement Days!

Date: _____
Time: _____
Place: _____

Please "bee" there!

Achievement Days

Fun with Children While Parents Serve

SERVICE & CITIZENSHIP

GOAL #2: Put on a Party to Entertain Children While Parents Serve

With your Achievement Days group, put on a Teddy Bear Party or other party to take care of the children in your ward or community while parents serve.

TEDDY BEAR PARTY PLANS: (1) Copy, color, and cut out stickers, tags, labels, and bear hat. (2) Gather supplies needed for the activities, snacks, and food. (3) Set table with plates, cups, and napkins, placing a name tag by each plate. (4) Set up games and activities and prepare food.

Teddy Bear Snack Sack

GAMES & ACTIVITIES: (1) Pin a name tag on each child. (2) Make a Teddy Bear's Snack Sack for each child. (3) Play Pin the Nose on the Bear. (4) Play Pin the Bee on the Bear's Nose. (5) Go Bear Paw Fishing. (6) Have a Teddy Bear Hug Relay. (7) Make a Teddy Bear Hat. (8) Serve Teddy Bear Food. (9) Decorate Teddy Bear Snack Sack.

TEDDY BEAR PARTY

Introduction:

Having a Teddy Bear party for children ages 3-6 can be quick-and-easy if you:
1. Follow the Before Party steps below.
2. Know how to use the party stickers, detailed on the right.
3. Following the party plans below.

Before Party:

Step #1: Copy, color, and cut out stickers, tags, labels, and bear hat for each child.
Step #2: Gather supplies. Notice that the items needed for the activities are <u>underlined</u>, and snack or food items needed are in a box.
Step #3: Set table with plates, cups, and napkins, placing a name tag by each plate.
Step #4: Set up activities and prepare food.

Three Ways to Use Party Stickers:

1. **Prizes for Games and Activities.**
2. **Table Decorations (below).**
3. **Teddy Bear Snack Sack Decorations.**
• <u>BEAR, BEAR'S NOSE, and BEE STICKERS:</u>
1. Give as prizes after the Pin the Nose on the Bear and the Pin the Bee on the Bear's Nose games.
2. Tape to a paper plate (folding the bear's chin and taping it under the plate as shown below).
3. After eating, remove from plate and glue on the Teddy Bear Snack Sack.
• <u>BEAR PAWS and FISH STICKERS:</u>
1. Give as prizes after the Bear Paw Fishing activity.
2. Tape paws on the bottom of the paper plate and fish on the cup.
3. After eating, remove from the plate and cup, and glue on the Teddy Bear Snack Sack.

Party Plans:

#1—PIN A NAME TAG ON EACH CHILD using a safety pin.

#2—TEDDY BEAR'S SNACK SACK:
1. Glue the Teddy Bear Snack Sack label on the top front of a <u>lunch sack</u> and the bear name tag on the back of sack for each child (shown left).

2. Write their name on the sack as they arrive. As the party progresses you will fill sack with snacks won for playing the games and activities, and decorate the sack at the end, with the stickers used for the table decorations.

#3—PIN THE NOSE ON THE BEAR:
1. Tell children about a bear's nose. Bears don't see very well so they have to use their nose to find things. They sniff out mice, fish, insects, nuts, plants, fruit, and honey to eat. Let's pretend we are a blind bear and put on our blindfolds and try to find the bear's nose.
2. Tape a bear to the wall in front of each child.
3. Have children take turns taping the nose on their bear while <u>blindfolded</u>. Have them stand 3-4 feet away from the bear, turn them around, and point them to the bear. Make sure double-stick tape is on the back of the nose.

4. The child who tapes the bear's nose the closest to the bear's nose in front of them wins an extra snack.
5. Treat children with cinnamon bears and graham cracker bears to eat or put on their plate or in their Teddy Bear's Snack Sack.

#4—PIN THE BEE ON THE BEAR'S NOSE:

1. Tell children that bears have a sweet tooth. When they smell honey in a beehive, they use their claws and paws to get the honey. When the bees catch them, they sting them on the nose. Let's pretend we are a bee and sting the bear on the nose.
2. Follow steps #1-4 <u>above</u>, except, tape a bee on the bear's nose instead.
3. Treat children to honey taffy.

#5—BEAR PAW FISHING:

1. Tell children that bears fish with their paws. They stand by a stream until a fish swims by, then they grab it with their paws, using their sharp claws to hold onto it. Let's pretend we are bears going fishing for our food.
2. Place a <u>large bowl</u> full of popcorn, goldfish crackers, and fish-shaped gummy candy.
3. Have children sit around bowl in a circle.
4. Tape the bear paw stickers on the top of their hands with double-stick tape.
5. Have children take turns reaching in the bowl to fish for snacks until the bowl is empty or their Teddy Bear Snack Sacks *are full.
6. Tape the bear paws on their plate and the fish on their cup (pages 106-107).

#6—TEDDY BEAR HUG RELAY:

1. Tell children that bear cubs love to play and hug each other. These are called bear hugs. We can give those we love a hug and hug our teddy bears, but we should never try to hug a real bear.
2. Line children up in two lines, facing <u>two chairs</u> across the room. Place <u>two teddy bears</u> on chairs.
3. At the word "go" children at the front of the line on both teams race to the chair in front of them, pick up the teddy bear, and give it a big bear hug. Then, they race to the back of the line and the next player does the same thing. The first team to finish the race wins an extra snack.
4. Give children some Hershey's Hugs candies to place in their Teddy Bear Snack Sack.

#7—TEDDY BEAR HAT:
Children can help you make this hat (shown right), put it on, and pretend they are walking through the forest looking for mice, fish, insects, nuts, plants, fruit, and honey to eat. Option: Tape bear paw stickers on the tops of their hands to wear as they crawl.
To Make Hat: Fit headband to child's head with a <u>fastener</u> (safety pin or sticky-back Velcro) and glue on the front the teddy bear's head.

#8—TEDDY BEAR FOOD (on <u>plates and cups</u> decorated with stickers):

• **FISH STICKS:** Tell children that bears love to eat fish. They go to the streams, wait for the fish, and then grab them with their paws and claws to eat. Serve them precooked fish sticks.

• **BEAR'S HONEY BUTTER ON CRACKER (with Gummy Worm):** Tell children that bears have a sweet tooth. They climb trees to find beehives and honey. They also dig in the ground and bark of the trees to find insects, using their claws to grab and eat them. Serve honey butter on crackers, topped with an optional gummy worm. Mix a cup of butter with a cup of honey and blend until smooth. Place in a container and serve with a <u>knife</u> so children can spread some on crackers.

• **ANTS ON A LOG** (fill celery with peanut butter and top with raisins. Tell children that bears smell and dig for insects to eat, using their claws to dig them out of the ground or under the bark on trees.

• **TEDDY BEAR CUPCAKES** frosted and ready for children to decorate. Place large drops at the top for the ears, one for the nose, and licorice string for the mouth. Cut a large gumdrop in fourths or use candies for the eyes. Flatten out gumdrops used for the ears by rolling them in sugar and pressing with a rolling pin.

• **TEDDY BEAR MILK:** Serve milk in the cup and tell children that bear cubs get milk from their mothers.

#9—DECORATE TEDDY BEAR SNACK SACK (detailed in #2 on the previous page).

B

Teddy Bears!

A

I sure love

B

A

Teddy Bear
Snack Sack

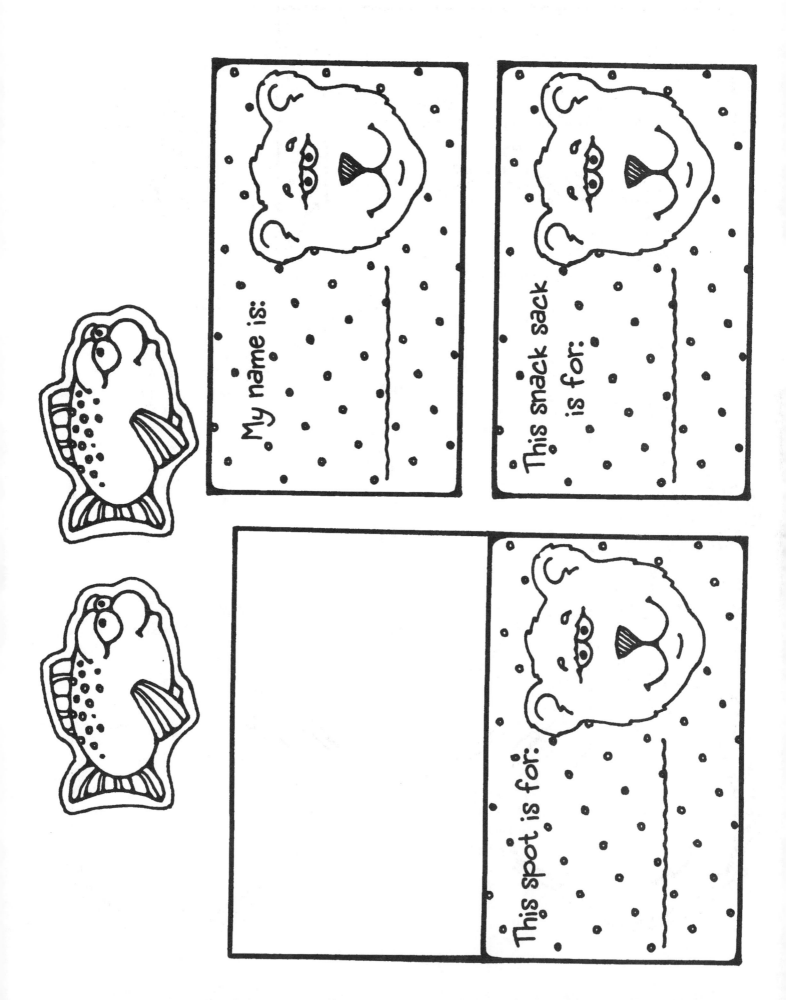

My name is:

This snack sack is for:

This spot is for:

SPIRITUALITY
Theme #1: Gospel Standards Help Me

Invitation: Copy-and-create invitation (page 109) to give girls a week before activity. Write items you need them to bring to decorate with Gospel Standards symbols*.

Icebreaker Activity: Review My Gospel Standards with Symbols

DO AHEAD: Copy the My Gospel Standards symbols (page 110) to complete the goal below onto colored cardstock paper for each girl. Supply a cardstock piece of paper and an Achievement Days booklet for each girl.

REVIEW STANDARDS USING THE GOSPEL STANDARDS SYMBOLS:

1. Show the Gospel Standard symbols and talk about each one, reviewing the back page of My Achievement Days booklet.
2. Create a Gospel Standards symbol object (see goal instruction sheet).

Goal #1 Activity:
Decorate a Hat or Object with My Gospel Standards Symbols

YOU'LL NEED: Copy of the goal card (page 109), My Gospel Standards symbols (page 110) on cardstock paper, paper punch, laminating clear Contact paper, markers, scissors, ribbon, needle and thread, and a fabric hat, belt, tie, box, or other object for each girl to decorate with symbols. ***Request items needed on invitation.**

ACTIVITY: See goal card (page 109) for details.

Success Snack: Gospel Standards Symbol Treats:

As you serve each treat, read the Gospel Standard that is represented by the symbol (on the tags).
IDEAS:

1. Apple Symbol (serve cut-up apples to dip in caramel sauce or peanut butter) .... Symbol #8
2. Lightbulb Symbol (serve a scoop of ice cream on a flat-bottomed cone, add candy face) .... Symbol #1
3. Heart Symbol (serve heart-shaped cookies) .... Symbol #3
4. Lip Symbol (serve chocolate candies wrapped in red foil) .... Symbol #2
5. Temple Symbol (serve temple mints) .... Symbol #11
6. Coin Symbol (serve chocolate coins wrapped in gold foil) .... Symbol #2

Achievement Days

SPIRITUALITY

GOAL #1: Decorate a Hat or Object with My Gospel Standards Symbols

Decorate a fabric hat, box, belt, tie, necklace, or other object with Gospel Standards symbols.

TO DECORATE A HAT OR OBJECT: Color and cut out the 11 Gospel Standards symbols.

1. If gluing on a box, cut out the square, and not the tag.

2. If sewing on an object (e.g., a hat), do the following:

• Cut out the symbol and words that match each symbol.

• Glue the symbol and words back-to-back.

• Laminate tags.

• Paper punch a hole where indicated in each tag.

• Tie a ribbon and bow through the hole.

• Sew the tag onto a hat, belt, tie, or ribbon, or other object.

NOTE: The meaning of each symbol is written on the back of each tag. Look at these often to help you memorize your Gospel Standards.

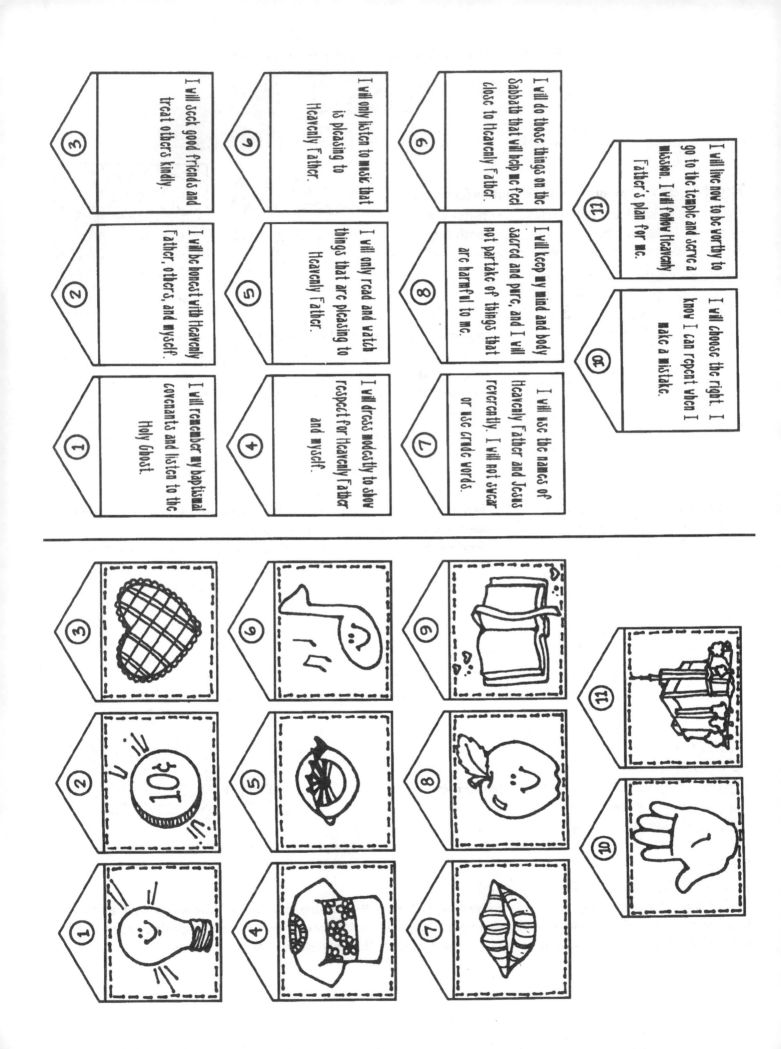

3. I will seek good friends and treat others kindly.

6. I will only listen to music that is pleasing to Heavenly Father.

9. I will do those things on the Sabbath that will help me feel close to Heavenly Father.

11. I will live now to be worthy to go to the temple and serve a mission. I will follow Heavenly Father's plan for me.

2. I will be honest with Heavenly Father, others, and myself.

5. I will only read and watch things that are pleasing to Heavenly Father.

8. I will keep my mind and body sacred and pure, and I will not partake of things that are harmful to me.

10. I will choose the right. I know I can repent when I make a mistake.

1. I will remember my baptismal covenants and listen to the Holy Ghost.

4. I will dress modestly to show respect for Heavenly Father and myself.

7. I will use the names of Heavenly Father and Jesus reverently. I will not swear or use crude words.

SPIRITUALITY

Theme #2: Sunday Fun Activities

Invitation: Copy-and-create invitation (page 112) to give girls a week before activity. Invitation asks girls to bring a large shoe box to create a Sabbath Day Activity Box and contact or wrapping paper to cover box.

Icebreaker Activity:
Brainstorm Sabbath Worthy Activities

DO AHEAD: Copy the Super Sunday Sabbath Day Activities (page 113) for each girl.

BRAINSTORM SABBATH DAY WORTHY ACTIVITIES: Read Exodus 20:8-11. Talk about the feelings you have when you are with your family and are engaged in Sabbath Day activities. Ask them to share activity ideas that have helped them keep to invite the Spirit on this special day. Talk about the importance of sharing this day with their family. Give each girl the Sabbath Day Activities list and a pencil.

1. Brainstorm first, having girls write their ideas on the back of the Super Sunday Sabbath Day Activities page.

2. Review the ideas found on the Super Sunday Sabbath Day Activities list.

3. Suggest that girls choose from these activities and write them on cards so they can post one or more each week to try.

Goal #2 Activity: Create a Sabbath Day Activity Box to Fill with Sabbath Fun

YOU'LL NEED: Copy of the goal card (page 112) and the Sabbath Day Activity Box label and stickers (page 114) for each girl. Gather contact, wrapping paper or acrylic paint, glue, scissors, and markers to create box.

ACTIVITY:

TO CREATE BOX: Cover box with contact or wrapping paper, or paint with paint. Glue the Sabbath Day Activity Box label on top and sunshine stickers around the box.

INCLUDE in the box the Super Sunday Sabbath Day Activities list (shown above). Also see the goal card (page 112), listing items you can put in the box. Encourage girls to meet with their family to include items that will help them keep the Sabbath day holy.

Success Snack: "Sun"day Cake.

With bright yellow frosting, frost a two-layer round cake with frosting in between. Use wafer cookies to stick them on the sides of the cake to make sun rays. Tell girls that they can have a sunny disposition each Sunday if they have their Sabbath Day Activity box with fun ideas they can share with their family.

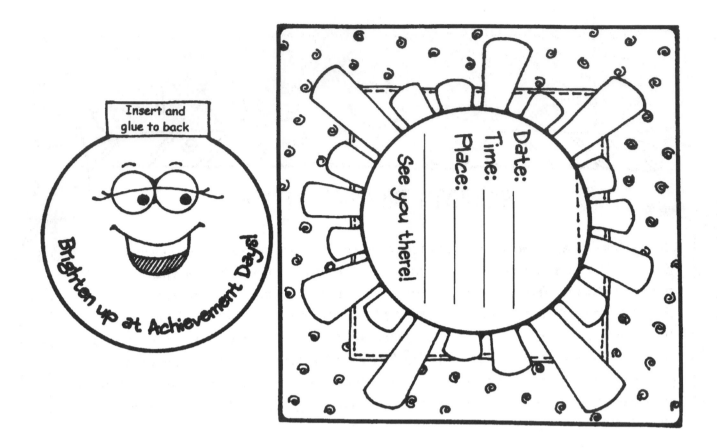

Insert and glue to back

Brighten up at Achievement Days!

Date:
Time:
Place:

See you there!

Achievement Days

Sunday Fun Activities

SPIRITUALITY

GOAL #2: Create a Sabbath Day Activity Box

Decorate a Sabbath Day Activity Box to fill with Sabbath day fun activities. Include one or more of the following items to help you keep the Sabbath day holy:

✿ scriptures and scripture marking pencils

✿ *Friend, Era, Ensign* magazines

✿ letter writing stationery   ✿ journal   ✿ goal plans

✿ addresses of friends, family, and elderly friends

✿ games to play with family, e.g., Jacks, Skipbo, Old Maid, Fish, memory games, and gospel games

✿ Hymns and Primary songs

✿ family home evening lesson ideas

✿ handouts from church and Achievement Days

✿ notepad and pen   ✿ cross-word and other puzzles

✿ list of family traditions and activities

✿ pictures and certificates to place in Book of Remembrance

Super Sunday

SABBATH DAY ACTIVITIES:

Have a family devotional where scriptures are read. Present a family home evening. Watch a Church video. Make ice cream sundaes. Write in journal. Sing hymns. Read and mark scriptures. Write letters to distant relatives and friends. Visit the elderly or shut-ins. Play games with family. Have scripture story and verse sharing time. Have a scripture chase. Read the Church magazines. Walk and appreciate nature. Pretend the Savior is visiting you in your home today. Play soft Sunday music. Have special family prayer where everyone says a prayer. Have a Sabbath day breakfast or enjoy a smoothie or milkshake while you read your favorite scripture or verse. Write or read family histories. Write to missionaries or distant friends. Practice reverence. Listen carefully to teachers and speakers and share what you learned. Use rest rooms and get drinks before meetings at church. Share flannel board stories. Make up and perform gospel puppet shows. Prepare treats together. Learn about foreign lands. Read family histories and learn about your family tree (generation by generation). Read articles in church magazines and report to family. Memorize hymns, Primary songs, Articles of Faith, and scriptures. Spend time with family (not friends). Spend quiet time in your room. Have individual prayers, asking for guidance and expressing thanks. Have a family secret pal you do things for on the Sabbath. Make up and give out good deed coupons to do service during the week. Write a family letter to each member and cut out pictures from magazines or draw pictures to put in letter. Make a family goal poster with pictures. Create picture puzzles by mounting on cardstock paper and cutting out in puzzle shapes. Create an indoor treasure hunt to search for Sabbath day treats (making up clues). Try old family recipes. Do dishes together. Write your testimonies and place in Book of Mormons with your picture to be given to investigators. Read *Children's Book of Mormon* and other stories from the standard works. Visit the sick. Learn and share pioneer stories of courage. Make get well and other greeting cards. Make a timeline, noting special events of your life. Write experiences you have had each year and share with family. Make up clues for scriptural characters to guess who is who. Rest. Write, call, or visit grandparents. Create paper dolls to teach and play with small children. Have a Sunday campfire meeting by sitting around a lit candle. Campfire Activities: Have a sing-along, learn old-fashioned songs, tell stories, read scriptures, share testimonies, and have s'mores melted in microwave.

SPORTS & PHYSICAL FITNESS

Theme #1: Be Heart Smart

Invitation: Copy-and-create invitation (page 116) to give to girls a week before activity.

Icebreaker Activity:

Learn 5 Heart-Smart Steps

DO AHEAD: Copy the Heart-Smart Exercise Workout chart (pages 117-118) on cardstock paper for each girl. Color and cut out a sample chart to show, gluing part A to part B. Come dressed to enjoy an exercise workout.

LEARN 5 HEART-SMART STEPS: Have an exercise expert/aerobics instructor talk to girls about the Heart-Smart Exercise Workout chart and why they should exercise to have a healthy heart. **IDEAS:** (1) Your heart is a muscle that needs to be exercised. Exercise helps your heart pump blood properly and gives you strength and energy. (2) People exercise for different reasons: to lose weight, create a healthy heart, increase mobility.

POINT TO CHART AND REVIEW:

♥ **OUT OF SHAPE HEART:** Say, "Do you lack energy and feel tired? After running a half a block, do you feel like you're going to die? Do you watch a lot of TV or play video games or computer games too much? If so, you might be out of shape."

♥ **WARM UP HEART:** Get your muscles going slowly with flowing exercises or stretches, not jumping. Start from the top of your head and move your head side to side, then shoulders, waist, legs, then feet. Stretch out on the floor, just enough to feel it; stop if it's painful.

♥ **PEAK HEART:** Start doing a cardiovascular exercise like jumping or jogging. Continue the exercise for 15-20 minutes to get your heart muscles pumping. Your resting heart rate when you first get out of bed is about 60-80 beats per minute; 140-170 is when you are in the middle (or peak) of your cardiovascular workout when your heart is pumping. The higher your resting heart rate, the worse shape you are in. Your heart is having to pump hard to get the blood to your body because it is not in good shape.

♥ **COOL DOWN HEART** is when you sweat the most, because your body trying to cool off. You should continue moving until your heart rate is down to 100 or below. Then you can sit down or rest. If you don't cool down before resting, you stress your heart and you can wear it out. ♥ **FIT HEART** comes from exercising 3-5 times a week.

Goal #1 Activity: Learn Heart-Smart Exercises.

YOU'LL NEED: Copy of the goal card, and Heart-Smart Exercise Workout chart (pages 116-118) for each girl. **ACTIVITY:** Have a 20-minute workout following the 5 steps of the Heart-Smart Exercise Workout. See goal card (page 116) for details. Ideas: Have a 5-minute warm up, a 20-minute workout, and a five-minute cool down, led by an expert (ideas on goal card).

Success Snack: Heart-Shaped Apple: Cut a red apple in half and take out the center. With a knife, cut each half into a heart shape. Tell girls that eating healthy foods makes for a healthy heart. Eat a balanced meal three times a day, don't eat more than you need to, avoid fried foods, drink 6-8 glasses of water a day, chew food well, and don't skip breakfast.

SPORTS & PHYSICAL FITNESS

GOAL #1: Learn Heart-Smart Exercises

Regular aerobic exercise may help lessen the risk of heart disease (D&C 89:20).

♥ Post the Heart-Smart Exercise Workout poster (shown left) to guide you in your workout. It shows what your heart looks like when it's out of shape and what steps to take to exercise properly: Warm-up, Stretch, Peak, Cool Down. The result is a Fit Heart.

♥ Choose one or more of the following heart-smart exercises and have a heart-smart workout: brisk walking, jogging, treadmill, stair-climbing, swimming, aerobic dance, jump rope, tennis, basket ball, soccer, water aerobics, step aerobics, bicycling, dancing, rowing, skating, or any exercise that gets the heart pumping for 20 minutes. Be sure to follow each of the heart-smart steps above, especially warming up and cooling down.

♥ To check your heart rate, find your pulse and count the beats for 10 seconds and multiply by 6. To find your minimum heart rate, subtract your age from 220 and then multiply by 0.60 (find maximum heart rate by multiplying by 0.90).

HEART RATE EXAMPLE: For a ten-year-old, the minimum while exercising is 220 - 10 = 210 x 6 = 1260 beats per minute (rounded off = 12 beats in 10 seconds); the maximum is 220 - 10 = 210 x 9 = 1890 beats per minute (rounded off = 19 beats in 10 seconds).

SPORTS & PHYSICAL FITNESS
Theme #2: Flip Over Old-Fashioned Games

Invitation: Copy-and-create invitation (page 120) to give to girls a week before activity. Parents or grandparents may be invited to join in on the fun.

Bounce on over to
Achievement Days
for some
Old Fashioned Fun!

Date: _____ Time: _____
Place: _____
_____

See you there!

Ice-breaker Activity:
Flip Through Game Book to Flip Over Old-Fashioned Fun!

Flip Over
Old Fashioned Games!

DO AHEAD: Copy the Flip Over Old-Fashioned Games book for each girl, cut out book, punch at top and place two metal rings through holes. Girls can take book home to color. Gather material to play games (e.g., jacks, empty can for Kick-the-Can, etc.).

ACTIVITY: Hand each girl a Flip Over Old-Fashioned Games book and flip through it together. Then assign games to different girls to review and present during the next activity (as girls play the selected games).

Goal #2 Activity: Learn Classic Games That Last Forever

YOU'LL NEED: Copy of the goal card (page 120) and a Flip Over Old-Fashioned Games book for each girl.
ACTIVITY: Play at least three old-fashioned games. See goal card (page 120) for details. See the hopscotch treat below that you can enjoy while you play a game of hopscotch (rules not listed in the book).

Success Snack: Three Choices: Favorite Game Cupcakes, Hopscotch Cookies, or Sports Party Mix

CHOICE #1: Favorite Game Cupcakes. Make and frost cupcakes. Have decorator frostings or puddings (to squeeze out of the corner of a zip-close bag) to decorate cupcakes. Have each girl decorate their cupcake with their favorite game they have played with family and friends.
CHOICE #2: Hopscotch Cookies. Use frosting from a tube to place numbers 1-8 on eight rectangular cookies. Display cookies a tray showing 1, 2, and 3 at the bottom, 4 and 5 side-by-side on top, then 6, then 7 and 8 on top of those. This game could be played as you eat, last using sidewalk chalk in the drive way. You'll need sidewalk chalk and a hoppy taw.
CHOICE #3: Sports Party Mix. Obtain sports-shaped crackers and candies available and mix together to serve in a bowl or with popcorn. You can purchase chocolate soccer balls wrapped in foil.

Bounce on over to
Achievement Days
for some
Old Fashioned fun!

Date: _____ Time: _____

Place: _____

See you there!

Achievement Days

SPORTS & PHYSICAL FITNESS

GOAL #2: Learn Classic Games that Last Forever

Learn how to play at least three classic games that have been entertaining children and adults for years. Try one with your friends or family.

CHOOSE FROM THOSE FOUND IN YOUR "FLIP OVER OLD-FASHIONED GAMES BOOK*, OTHER GAMES LISTED, OR THOSE SHARED BY PARENTS AND GRANDPARENTS:

*Flip Over Old Fashioned Game Book Games: Jacks, Fox and Geese, Kick-the-Can, Button, Button, Who Has the Button, Hot Potato, Musical Chairs, Charades, Red Light, Green Light, Spin-the-Bottle, Pass the Orange Relay, Balloon Battle, Sardines, Marco Polo, Red Rover, Mother, May I?

OTHERS: Old Maid, Go Fish, frisbee, hula-hoop, stilts, yo-yos, dominoes, checkers, Chinese Checkers (using marbles), Pick-up-Sticks, Monopoly, Flashlight tag, I Have a Little Doggy, jump rope rhymes, tic-tac-toe, hopscotch, and Duck, Duck, Goose.

Flip Over

Old Fashioned Games!

JACKS

Toss six jacks on the surface in one throw. With each attempt to pick up jack(s), toss the ball into the air while you pick up the jacks. If the ball bounces twice, it's the other player's turn. As long as you are picking up jacks without touching the other jacks, you can keep playing. ONES: Pick up one jack at a time, repeating six times. TWOS: Pick up two jacks at a time, repeating three times. THREES: Pick up three jacks at a time. FOURS: Pick up four jacks and then the last two. FIVES: Pick up five jacks and then the last one. SIX: Pick up all six jacks at once. The first to complete this wins! HINT: When you start with ones you want to scatter them so they don't touch. When you are picking up groups (e.g., fours, fives, or sixes) you want to toss them in such a way that they stay more close together.

KICK-THE-CAN:

1. Play in a yard with many hiding places. Place an empty can in the center of the yard and form a 5-foot circle around the can.
2. The player chosen as It stands in the circle while the other players try to catch him off guard. When they do, they rush in to kick the can as far as they can before It tags them. While It rushes to put the can back on the spot, the others run to hide.
3. Once the can is on the spot It yells "Freeze!" All players must stop where they are. It calls all players in sight, making them stand in the circle on one leg. It then searches for the others who can at any moment kick the can, freeing all the prisoners. It must put the can back while the others hide. It can then yell "Freeze" again, repeating the process. IT REMAINS IT UNTIL It can't find any prisoners after yelling "Freeze." Then anyone hiding can kick the can and yell "Home Free." Then all players, including It, runs for the circle. The last one to enter the circle becomes It for the next round.

Flip Over

Old Fashioned Games!

FOX AND GEESE:

Make a large circle path in the snow, then crisscross (like cutting a pie) to create trails leading into the center, or safety zone. The fox tries to catch the geese. The geese are safe in the center. But they can't stay there more than five seconds. If caught, the goose changes places with the fox. All players have to have at least one foot on the path or the center at all times.

HOT POTATO:

OPTION #1: Give players one or two hot potatoes (wrapped in foil) to toss while standing in a circle. When the potato is dropped by a player that player is out.

If it's a large circle, use two potatoes. Keep playing over and over.

You could say "hot" each time you toss the potato.

OPTION #2: Players sit in a circle, cross-legged and toss the hot potato back and forth. If the potato is dropped, the last player who touched it must fetch and toss it.

CHARADES:

Write short phrases on slips of paper that represent a person, place, thing, book, movie, or song. Divide players into two teams and explain that they are to draw a phrase and give silent clues to their team to guess the phrase. They may use the following clues to tell if it is a person (point to the top of your head), place (look into the distance), thing (hold out hand in cup shape), book (open hands like a book), movie (pretend to run a video camera), song (wave hand across open mouth). TO PLAY: A player from each team takes a turn drawing a phrase from the container and giving nonverbal clues. Your team has only three minutes to guess, then the other team has a chance to guess for three minutes. Give one point for each phrase guessed. If the second team does not guess, go on to the next team. The following motions can also be clues: cup your hand behind your ear means "sounds like"; for "first word" or "second word," hold up one or two fingers.

BUTTON, BUTTON, WHO HAS THE BUTTON:

You'll need a button.

1. Sit players in a circle on the floor, giving one player a button who becomes the leader.

2. Players put their hands together in prayer position, and leader holds the button inside hands, also in prayer position.

3. Leader stands inside circle and walks from person to person, slipping fingers through each player's hands, then secretly drops the button into one person's hands.

4. The leader says, "Button Button Who Has the Button?"

5. Everyone except the leader guesses. The person who guesses correctly, becomes the new leader and repeats the process.

MUSICAL CHAIRS:

Set up chairs in a circle two feet apart with chairs facing inward. There should be enough for all players except one. Have players parade outside the chairs while you play music. One person monitors the music and chairs while you play music. When the music stops, players scramble for a seat. The player left standing leaves the game and a chair is taken out of the circle.

That player who is out could monitor the music for the next round.

MARCO POLO

Marco Polo is a swimming game. Marco Polo is chosen to close their eyes and count to 10. The others scatter around the pool within 4 feet of Marco Polo. After 10, Marco Polo swims with eyes closed to tag the other players calling out

"Marco." The other players must within five seconds yell

"Polo," so Marco can tag them. When another player

is tagged, they become Marco Polo.

MOTHER, MAY I?:

A player is selected to be the "mother." Players line up in a row, 20 feet away facing mother. Mother calls out instructions to each player, calling by name, saying, for example, "Jenny, take four giant steps." Player must say, "Mother, may I?" before advancing. If players forget, they return to the starting line. If player says, "Mother, may I?" then "mother" might say "yes you may" or "no you may not." If "yes" player steps forward; if mother says "no you may not... take four hops instead," then player follows instructions Player must say, "Mother, may I?" or be sent back. The first player to cross behind "mother" and back to the starting line wins.

SARDINES:

Play in the house in the dark. One player hides while the other players count to 20.

All players look for the person who is hiding. When the seeker finds the person

hiding they hide with them in the same spot. As each player

finds the hiding place, they join them quietly,

until the last person joins the group.

The first person who finds the hiding

place is the one who hides the next time.

RED ROVER:

Divide into two teams who face each other 10 feet apart. Players in each team hold hands. One player from a team calls out a player's name from the opposite team, saying, "Red Rover, Red Rover, send "Jenny" right over. Jenny then runs at full speed to the other side to break through the arms of two players. If that player does not break through they must stay on the opposing team's side. If they do break through they can take back a player from the opposing them over to their side. The game ends when one player is left on their team.

SPIN-THE-BOTTLE:

Option #1: Fill a bottle with fun things to do. e.g., "rub your head and tummy at the same time," "skip backwards," "make a sound like a chicken," "crawl like a snake to the door."

Option #2: Players make up things to do as you go along. To Play: Players sit in a circle. One starts out spinning the bottle. When the neck of the bottle points to someone, that person draws a funny action from the bottle, or the person who spun the bottle asks them to do something funny. That person does the action and then spins for the next person. If the bottle points to him/herself, the person on their left requests the funny action.

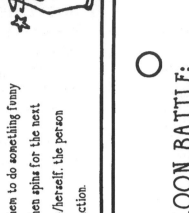

BALLOON BATTLE:

Have each player blow up a balloon and tie it to their ankle with a string. At "go," players race to stomp on the other person's balloons to burst them. When player's balloon is popped, player stays in the game and tries to get others' balloons. The last person to keep his balloon wins! You can play this in teams, giving each team a different-colored balloon. Play in teams, trying to win the battle.

RED LIGHT, GREEN LIGHT:

One player is the "Spot"light at the opposite end of the room while the others line up 40 feet away. The "Spot"light turns head, not looking at other players as she calls out either "red light" or "green light." When "Spot"light says "green light" players can walk (not run) toward the "Spot"light. When "Spot"light says "red light" the players must freeze before "Spot"light turns a back to the starting line. The first player to reach back to the starting line. The first player to reach "Spot"light can be the "Spot"light.

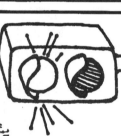

PASS THE ORANGE RELAY:

Divide into two teams with an orange for each team. There are two ways to play:

(1) FAST PACED: Standing up, hand the orange from the first person in the line to the next until it reaches the back. Then start over and pass it back. The first team to pass it up and back wins. If orange is dropped, start over with the first person.

(2) SLOW PACED: Pass the orange with players' feet sitting on chairs in a line; if dropped start over.

Buttons and Bows Daddy-Daughter Date

INVITATION AND STATIONERY:

1. Copy two invitations on page 127 (one for the dad and one for the daughter).

2. Copy the two pages of stationery: "I'm so glad that you're my dad," and "I'm so glad that you're my daughter!"

2. To Make Invitation: Fold Buttons and Bows tab and glue to the back of the invitation.

3. Paper punch top and bottom and lace a ribbon through to close, tying a bow on top.

4. Deliver Stationery: Deliver two weeks ahead, with the invitation, the stationery (pages 128-129) that reads: "I'm so glad that you're my daughter!" and "I'm so glad that you're my dad!" Pick up each letter before the activity without the other knowing. Cut out the stationery before delivering.

5. After gathering the stationery, make the Buttons and Bows Napkin and Utensil Holder using the personalized letter. See Table Decorations.

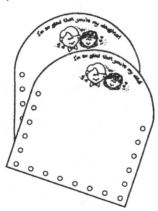

AS GUESTS ARRIVE:

1. Prepare and have ready to hand each dad and daughter their own personalized Buttons and Bows napkin and utensil holder (with the personal letter on the back). See Table Decorations to make.

2. Have guest find a place at the table by their place cards. See Decorations below.

BUTTONS AND BOWS MENU:

Serve the following: spaghetti, garlic bread, green salad, and Buttons and Bows Cupcakes. <u>Buttons and Bows Cupcakes</u>: Frost a cupcake for each dad and daughter. Decorating the dad's cupcake with a gumdrop buttons (roll large gumdrops flat and pierce two holes with a straw). Decorate the daughter's cupcake with an eatable bow (rolling two large gumdrops flat and cutting into strips, then tying into a bow, placing a 1/4" gumdrop ball in the center of the bow.

DECORATIONS:

• BUTTONS AND BOWS NAPKIN AND UTENSIL HOLDER:

1. Copy two Buttons and Bows envelopes on page 130 (one for the dad and one for the daughter).

2. Attach this envelope to the back of the dad and daughter letter (see Invitation).

3. Punch holes where indicated on both sides.

4. With two different pieces of ribbon or yarn, sew part A and B together, tying a bow in the center bottom.

• BUTTON AND BOW PLACE CARDS:

Copy, color and cut out a button place card for each dad and a bows place card for each daughter (pages 128-129).

2. Ahead of time, write each dad and daughter's name on a place card.

3. Fold like a tent card and place above each dad's and daughter's place setting.

• BUTTONS AND BOWS BALLOONS:

Tie a helium-filled balloon by each dad and daughter's chair. At the top (6-inches below balloon) tie a button on the dad's balloon and a bow on the daughters. These will be tied to wrists during dance. See Buttons and Bows Balloon Dance activity below.

GAMES AND ACTIVITIES:

• BUTTON UP RELAY RACE:

1. Divide dads and daughters evenly into two teams.
2. Have teams stand across the room with two large cardigan sweaters for the dads and two medium-sized sweaters for the daughters at the other end on a chair.
3. Count the buttons to make sure there is an equal number; if not, have them button one less.
4. At "go" a dad and a daughter from each team races to put on sweater, button it up, un-button the sweater and take it off. Then back. The next daddy and daughter race. The first team to finish wins! Give the winning team a cookie or gumdrop button.

• BUTTON, BUTTON WHO HAS THE BUTTON:

You'll need a button.

1. Sit daughters in a circle on the floor and dads stand behind daughters.
2. Give one girl a button, who becomes the leader.
3. Girls hold their hands in prayer position.
4. Leader walks from person to person and runs her fingers through each player's hands, holding onto the button (in prayer position). Leader secretly drops the button into one player's hand and then stands back. Have the leader pretend to drop the button in several hands before standing back.
5. The DADS GUESS WHERE THE BUTTON WENT. The first dad to guess the right girl wins.
6. His daughter now becomes the leader and repeats the process.

• BOW BEAUTY SHOP AND SPIKE BARBER SHOP:

<u>BOW BEAUTY SHOP</u>. Have daughters sit on chairs in a circle facing each other while dads stand behind with a comb and five bows (with bobby pins attached) and two fabric-covered elastics. Give dads 10 minutes to come up with the best hairstyle they can for their daughter telling them that they must use all five bows. Judge the prettiest, most unusual, and funniest hairstyles. Prize could be a pretty barrette.

<u>SPIKE BARBER SHOP</u>. Have dads sit on chairs in a circle facing each other while daughters restyle their dad's hair spiking it with gel. After 5 or 10 minutes give a prize for the coolest, most unusual, and the funniest style. Prize could be a bottle of styling gel.

• BUTTONS AND BOWS BALLOON DANCE:

Have dads and daughters take the balloon from their chair and tie it to their wrist as they dance with their daughters for the remaining time.

You're invited to a

Buttons and Bows

Daddy-Daughter date!

Date: _____ Time: _____

Place: _____

See you there!

Punch holes and close with ribbon.

Fold and glue tab to back.

Buttons and Bows

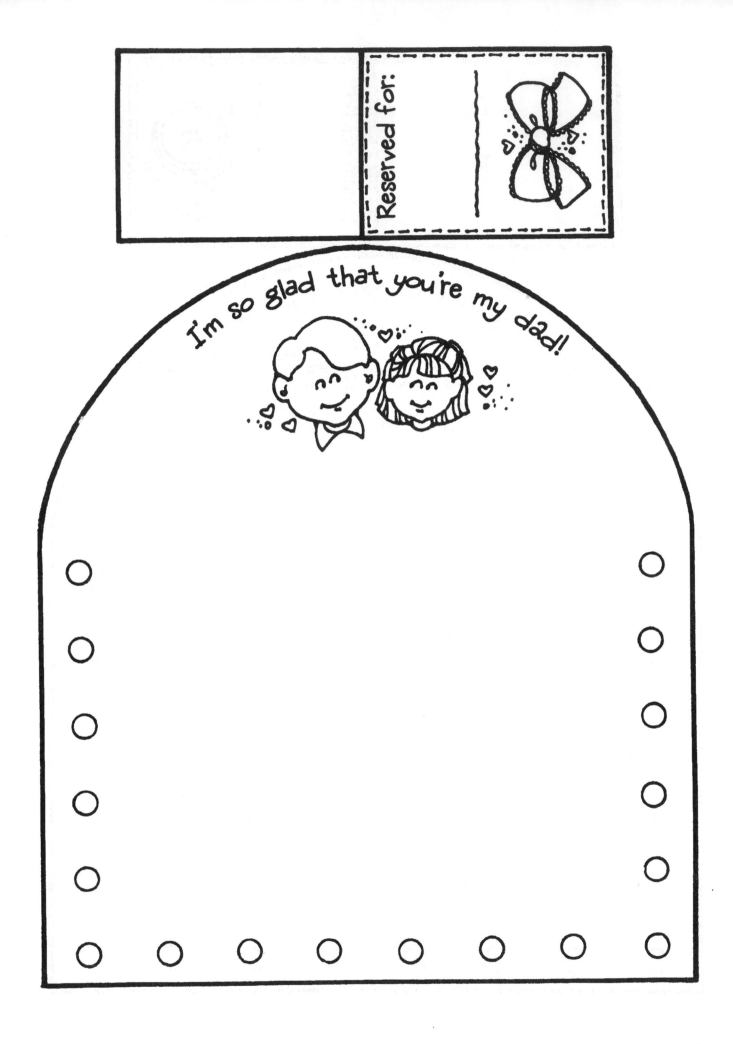

Reserved for:

I'm so glad that you're my dad!

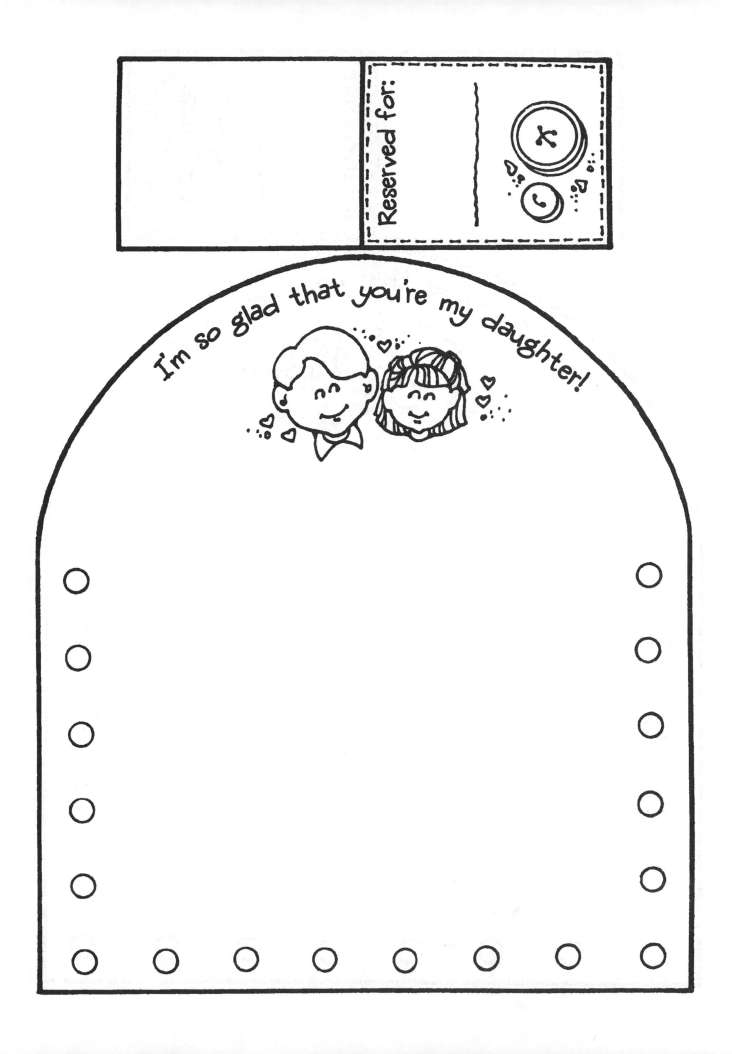

Reserved for:

I'm so glad that you're my daughter!

Dress and Dazzle! Mom and Me Fashion Show

You'll Need: Copies of invitation (page 132) for each mother/daughter, fashion look cards (page 133), menu items, and cookie pattern (page 134) for each mother/daughter.

DO AHEAD:

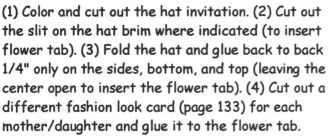

•INVITATIONS: Have girls make and deliver invitations to their moms.

TO MAKE:

(1) Color and cut out the hat invitation. (2) Cut out the slit on the hat brim where indicated (to insert flower tab). (3) Fold the hat and glue back to back 1/4" only on the sides, bottom, and top (leaving the center open to insert the flower tab). (4) Cut out a different fashion look card (page 133) for each mother/daughter and glue it to the flower tab. (5) Insert the tab in the slit in the hat so each girl and mother can pull out the tab to know their fashion look. (6) Fill in invitation and write the name of the narrator and the date the script is due on the invitation.

• GATHER FASHION SHOW SCRIPTS:

Have narrator gather scripts and make up the program ahead of time, listing the order of the participants and the fashion look.

> **HIPPIE SIXTIES LOOK.** IDEAS: Wear long hair, tie-dyed shirts, psychedelic (bright-colored) pants, flower crowns, pink lense wire glasses, love-bead necklace, and leather sandals. Say "Hey, dude!" "What's happenin'!" "Groovy." Snap fingers and recite a poem beatnik style.

• SET UP tables near the stage with a microphone.

• DECORATE TABLES AND STAGE with "fashion" themes. Delegate this to girls.

• MAKE FASHION SUGAR COOKIES ready to frost, using clothing patterns (page 134) to cut out: T-shirt, pants, skirt, vest, hat. Provide a variety of colored frosting, decorator candies, wooden craft sticks (to frost with), and paper plates to hold cookies.

SCHEDULE:

1. FILL OUT WHO'S WHO CARDS: As they arrive have them write on a card their name and something about them that no one else knows about and place the card in a container. Example: "I ate a live grasshopper when I was a toddler."

2. SERVE FOOD (see MENU).

3. SPOTLIGHT WHO'S WHO: As they eat have someone come up and draw the cards from the container and read the cards one at a time. Have others guess who it might be; then have them stand up or come up and give any details about the experience. Example: "My aunt said as I was eating the grasshopper, it was squirming for its life!"

4. HAVE FASHION SHOW: Narrator reads the script that the mothers and daughters have written, asking two mothers and daughters to come up one at a time. Guests can watch the fashion show from their tables. If time, narrator could give fashion tips.

5. DECORATE FASHION COOKIES to eat and take home. Have mother and daughter frost clothing shaped cookies with wooden craft sticks using different colored frostings. Decorate with candies.

MENU: Main Dish Idea #1: Chicken and Rice Salad over lettuce, served with a dinner roll and butter. Main Dish Idea #2: Serve the Chicken and Rice Salad inside a large croissant roll.

Serve lemonade with a straw adding a maraschino cherry and a half slice of a lemon. Fashion Cookies (see activity above).

> **CHICKEN AND RICE SALAD: Serve on top of Shredded Boston Lettuce.**
>
> **CHICKEN AND RICE SALAD:**
> **INGREDIENTS:** 1 box Uncle Ben's Wild Rice mix (made according to package directions). Juice of 1 lemon (or 2 tablespoons lemon juice), 3 cooked chicken breasts, cut into small cubes, 4 chopped green onions, 1 diced red bell pepper, 3 oz. pea pods, 2 medium cubed avocados*, 1 cup chopped pecans* or cashews.
> **TO MAKE:** Combine all except the avocado and pecans. Toss with DRESSING (below) and refrigerate 4-12 hours or a day ahead. *Before serving add avocados and pecans.
> **DRESSING** for Chicken and Rice: 2 cloves of crushed garlic, 1 T Dijon or brown mustard, ½ tsp. salt, 1/4 tsp. sugar, 1/4 tsp. pepper, 1/3 cup rice or red wine vinegar, 1/3 cup olive oil. Blend in blender.

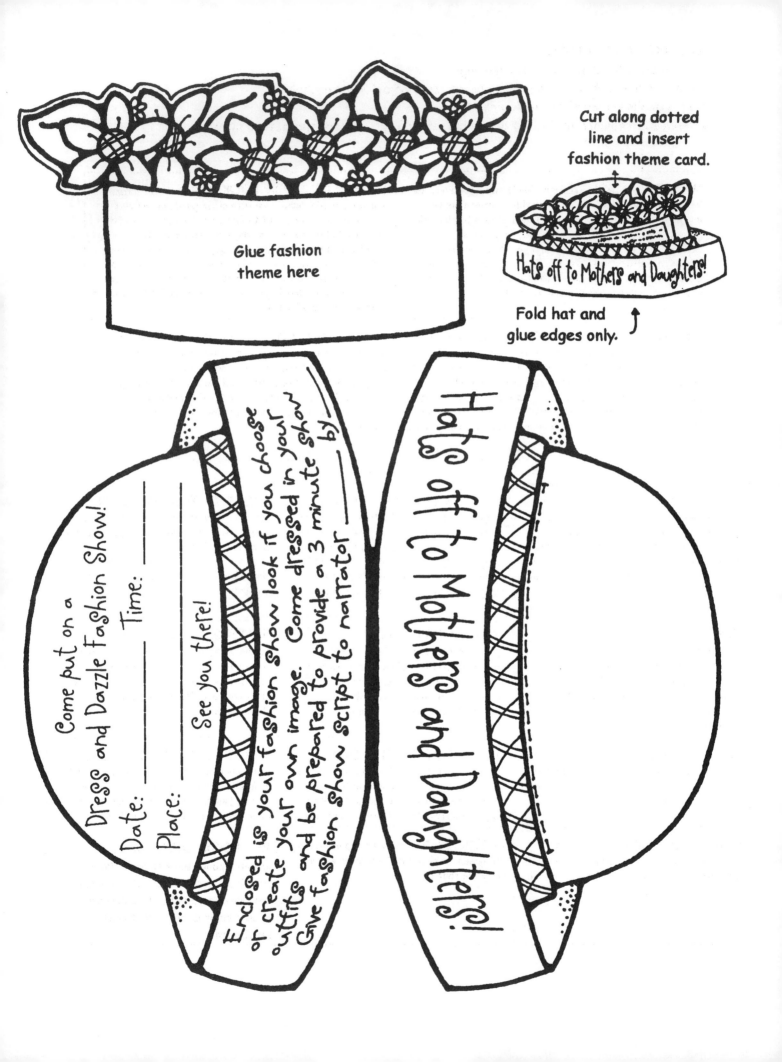

Glue fashion theme here

Cut along dotted line and insert fashion theme card.

Hats off to Mothers and Daughters!

Fold hat and glue edges only.

Come put on a Dress and Dazzle Fashion Show!

Date: _____

Time: _____

Place: _____

See you there!

Enclosed is your fashion show look if you choose or create your own image. Come dressed in your outfits and be prepared to provide a 3 minute show by _____. Give fashion show script to narrator.

Hats off to Mothers and Daughters!

TO MAKE INVITATION:
1. See instructions on the invitation page.
2. Cut out the fashion show scripts below (cutting off the border).
3. Glue on flower card for each girl.
4. Then slip the card in the hat invitation (after cutting along the dotted lines).

WESTERN LOOK. IDEAS: Say "Howdy, pardner!" as you enter stage. Wear western clothing, carry a pie tin, drink out of a canning jar or water jug, wear a bandana tied around your neck, wear a cowgirl hat, ride a stick horse, carry or look at a "Wanted" poster, eat trail mix, sew fringe to pants or vest, and say "Let's go rustle up some grub or cattle," or "Yip-peee!" as you leave. Dance a western line dance or swing to some country twang!

CLOWN OR HOBO LOOK. IDEAS: Wear a funny hairstyle or wig, paint face with clown paint, wear a red nose (use red ball and cut to fit), bright-colored, polka-dot or striped clothing that is baggy, big shoes, striped or colorful socks, huge flower corsage, a plunger around your neck, have one pant leg rolled up, use a toothbrush for a barrette, ride in a funny car (made out of cardboard). Do tricks, fall down, laugh, joke, and clown around. Carry lots of toys, e.g., a hoola-hoop, ball.

DETECTIVE - I SPY LOOK. IDEAS: Wear a trench coat or coat with collar turned up, dark glasses, carrying a spy glass and note pad with pencil to write clues. Have clues scattered across stage for you to find and identify, e.g., lipstick, obituary page from newspaper, key, book of matches, fingerprints, books, etc. Carry a Mystery Mansion or Clue game, or sit down and pretend to play game.

EGYPTIAN LOOK. IDEAS: Flat shoes, lots of gold jewelry, wide bracelets, jewelry in hair and on arms, wide collars, straight bangs, robes, scarf headbands across bangs, scarf over head with jewel head band over bangs, beaded collar, carry pottery. Or try the MUMMY LOOK: Wrap yourself in white strips of cloth, paper towels, or tissue.

BABY LOOK. IDEAS: Wear pajamas, using a pacifier and baby bottle on a string around your neck, saying, "Go-go Da-da, Ma-ma." Carry toys, cry, and drink your bottle. If you can find an extra large baby bottle bring that. Sing songs like "Twinkle, Twinkle Little Star," or "Lull-a-by Baby in the Treetops."

PIRATE LOOK. IDEAS: Wear a striped shirt, capris, flip-flops, or sandals (or go barefoot), head wrapped with a scarf, using props, e.g., a treasure chest, fake gold coins, money, jewelry, or edible jewelry, treasure map, and sing "Yo-ho-ho and a bottle of pop!" Walk the plank (board on the floor).

GREAT OUTDOORS LOOK. IDEAS: Wear shorts, T-shirts, tennis shoes, and carry binoculars, a jar to catch bugs, eat trail mix, large fake bug for necklace, hold pictures of birds on a dowel, throw gummy worms or fish crackers at the audience.

HIPPIE SIXTIES LOOK. IDEAS: Wear long hair, tie-dyed shirts, psychedelic (bright-colored) pants, flower crowns, pink lense wire glasses, love-bead necklace, and leather sandals. Say "Hey, dude!" "What's happenin'!" "Groovy." Snap fingers and recite a poem beatnik style.

PAJAMA PARTY LOOK. IDEAS: PJ's of course, sleeping bags, curlers, cardboard pizza (to show), favorite board games, favorite movie, popcorn necklace or carry a bag of popcorn, toothbrush, toothpaste, hairbrush, suitcase.

FIFTIES LOOK. IDEAS: Wear a poodle skirt, T-shirt, pony tail with scarf tied at top, white socks with canvas shoes, hold a record, model to 50s music, dance the jitter-bug (like the western swing), chew and blow bubble gum.

BARBIE DOLL LOOK. IDEAS: Dress up like a Barbie and Ken doll, use Barbie and Ken dolls for props. Make a cardboard car to drive in (wagon inside). Make up a story.

HAWAIIAN BEACH LOOK. IDEAS: Wear a modest swim suit, Hawaiian lei, or fish necklace, sandals or flip-flops, carry a towel, beach ball, sandbox items, e.g., rope shovel, bucket, beach umbrella.

BEAUTY SHOP LOOK. IDEAS: Wear curlers or have a ratted hairdo, lots of lipstick, bright nail polish, false eyelashes, junk jewelry, carry a hair dryer, wear a brush or comb as a necklace.

BABY DOLL LOOK. IDEAS: Walk real stiff with arms stiff and head jerking left and right. Wear your favorite costume and make up a story to fit.

ROYALTY: IDEAS: Dress up like a king and queen, or prince and princess. Act out a fairytale that fits.

PET LOOK. IDEAS: Dress up wearing paper ears to look like a dog or rabbit, fish, or cat. Imitate the cat, making sounds. Have narrator read a poem about your favorite pet/animal.

COOKIE
PATTERNS

Quarterly Motivation and Award Activities

Every 3 months have one of the following goal motivation activities, inviting girls and parents.
Enjoy the goal activities, give out award certificates, and enjoy a Success Snack.

Theme #1: Fishing for Success!

Invitation: Copy-and-create invitation (page 136) to give to girls a week ahead.
Encourage them to invite their parents to attend.

Icebreaker Activity – Go Fishing for Success!
OBJECTIVE: Learn 12 ways to accomplish their goals.
YOU'LL NEED: Four sets of the #1-12 GO FISH cards (pages 136-137) on colored
cardstock paper. Four sets will make a deck if 6 girls are playing. (Or print colored
cards from CD-ROM on white cardstock paper). Make additional sets if more than
6-8 girls are playing.
TO MAKE GAME: Cut out cards and shuffle.
TO PLAY GAME: (see rules on #1-12 fish card pages).

FAVOR: "Tackle Your Goals"
Fish Tackle Box:
YOU'LL NEED: One Tackle Your Goals box
(page 140), two sets of Achievement Days goal cards (page 139), and four
sets of #1-12 GO FISH cards and rules (pages 137-138) for each girl to
place in box.
TO MAKE: Color, cut out tackle box, and fold where indicated. Glue sides to
make an envelope and enclose cards: 2 sets of Achievement Days goal cards
and GO FISH game.
TACKLE YOUR GOALS ACTIVITY: Tell girls that if they are going to
tackle their goals, they will need to write them down as well as the steps to
achieve each goal. BRAINSTORM: Write goal ideas for the 12 Achievement
Days areas on a poster or board. Then write the steps to achieve several of
them. Have girls write on their 24 fish goal cards (shown right) goals they
wish to achieve (2 cards for each Achievement Days area). Have them write
the steps for each goal. Place these in their tackle box to take out, post on their mirror or wall or in planner.
Suggest to girls that they review their goals often and "tackle" them one step at a time.

Great Catch! Award Certificate:

YOU'LL NEED: Copies of the Great Catch! certificate (page 136) for each girl.
TO MAKE CERTIFICATE: Color and cut out certificates, add their name and have
their leader sign cnd date the certificate.
AWARD CERTIFICATE PRESENTATION: Talk to each leader
ahead of time to learn specific goals the girls have achieved
the past three months. Ask several girls from each class to
show or tell about what they have done, then award
certificates.

Success Snacks (Fish Food): Fish crackers, gummy fish, gummy worms, small tuna
sandwich cut into fish shapes. Serve on fish plate. TO MAKE FISH PLATE: Option #1: Trace
fish pattern on a paper plate and cut out. Paper punch a hole through the eye. Option #2: Copy on cardstock paper
and cut out and glue fish on to a paper plate.

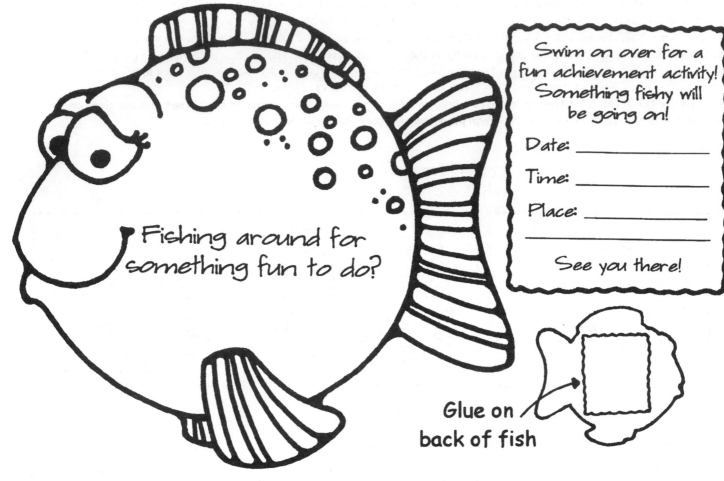

Fishing around for something fun to do?

Swim on over for a fun achievement activity! Something fishy will be going on!

Date: _____

Time: _____

Place: _____
_____

See you there!

Glue on back of fish

Great Catch!

Certificate of Achievement awarded to

_____

for fishing with success and achieving her goals.

_____   _____
Achievement Day Leader   Date

RULES FOR "GO FISHING FOR SUCCESS" GAME:

Sit in a circle with 4-6 players. Deal five fish cards to each player, placing the rest of the cards face down in the center. Players take turns asking another player for the card they need. For example, one player might say to another, "Jenny, do you have any threes?" If Jennie has them, she hands them over. If not, she would say, "Go fish," and the player draws a card from the center pile. Players can continue to play as long as they get the cards they ask for. But once they are asked to "go fish," their turn is over. Each time players collect a set of four matched cards (or a book), they lay the book in front of them. Each time a book is made, have girls read the fish card aloud to share the success idea.

TWO WAYS TO WIN: (1) When there are no more "go fish" cards, count the number of books (set of 4 matching cards). The player with the most books wins. (2) When player has no more fish cards left in her hand.

Copy 4 for each set of cards.

Get up every morning with a smile on your face. Every day is a new start!

Write down a plan before you start your goal.

Set a date when you will achieve your goal.

Plan your goal step by step.

Write each step on a calendar to help you accomplish your goal on time.

If at first you don't succeed, fish, fish again! Don't ever give up.

Copy 4 for each set of cards.

To see your progress, check off completed steps.

Take the plunge! Dive into your goals with enthusiasm.

Tell someone about your goals so they can offer support or help.

Picture in your mind how great you'll feel when you accomplish your goal.

Review your goal plan each day.

Pray for strength to complete your goal. Heavenly Father wants you to succeed!

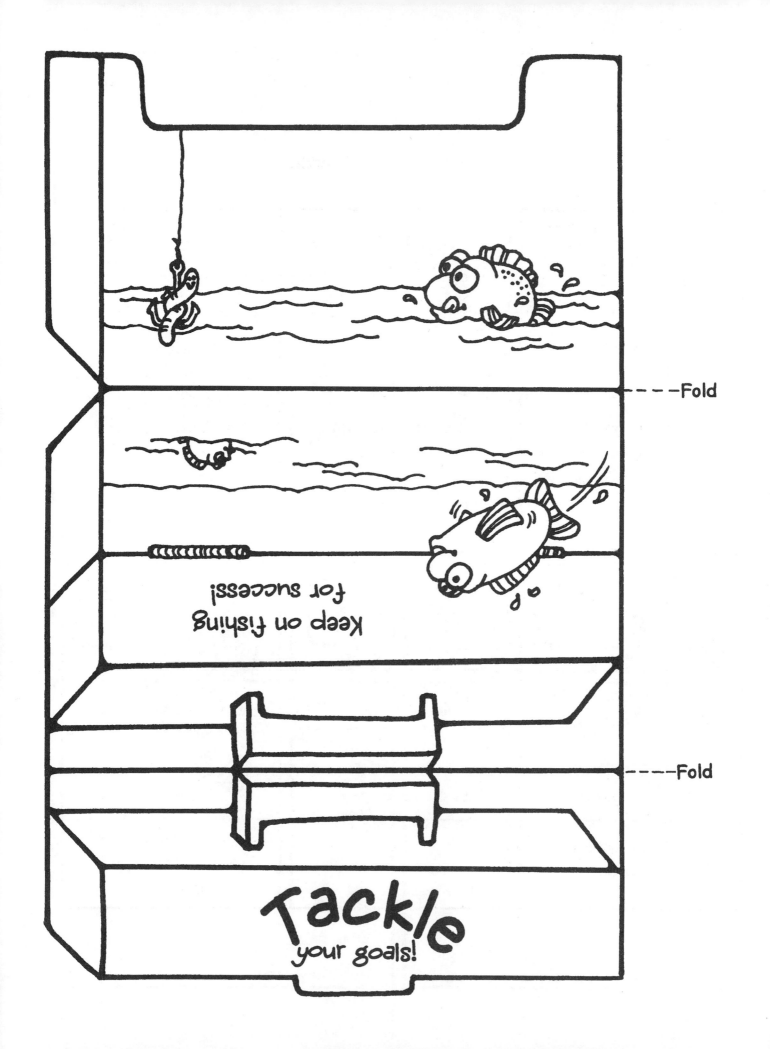

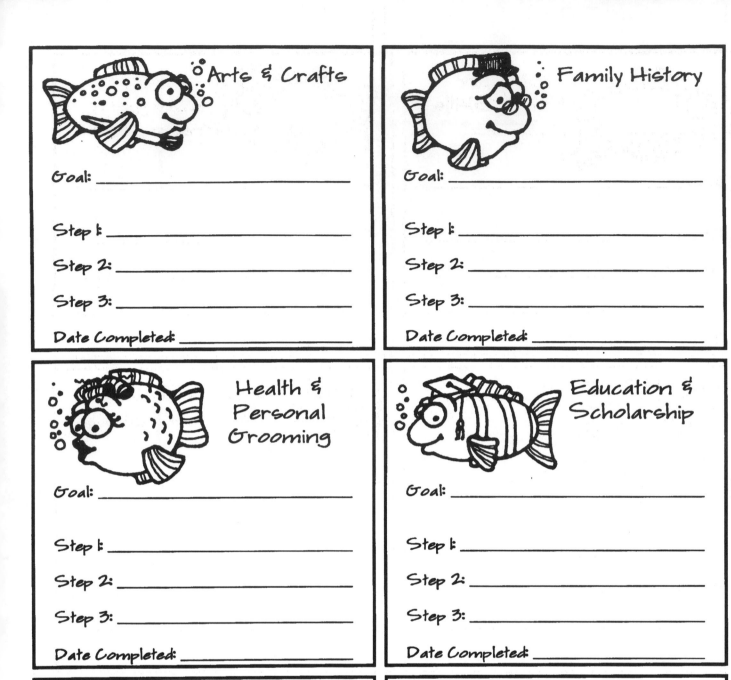

Arts & Crafts

Goal: _____

Step 1: _____

Step 2: _____

Step 3: _____

Date Completed: _____

Family History

Goal: _____

Step 1: _____

Step 2: _____

Step 3: _____

Date Completed: _____

Health & Personal Grooming

Goal: _____

Step 1: _____

Step 2: _____

Step 3: _____

Date Completed: _____

Education & Scholarship

Goal: _____

Step 1: _____

Step 2: _____

Step 3: _____

Date Completed: _____

Family Skills

Goal: _____

Step 1: _____

Step 2: _____

Step 3: _____

Date Completed: _____

Hospitality

Goal: _____

Step 1: _____

Step 2: _____

Step 3: _____

Date Completed: _____

Outdoor Fun & Skills

Goal: _____

Step 1: _____

Step 2: _____

Step 3: _____

Date Completed: _____

Safety & Emergency Preparedness

Goal: _____

Step 1: _____

Step 2: _____

Step 3: _____

Date Completed: _____

Spirituality

Goal: _____

Step 1: _____

Step 2: _____

Step 3: _____

Date Completed: _____

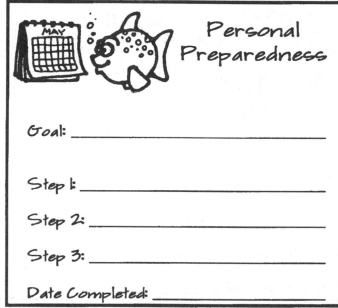

Personal Preparedness

Goal: _____

Step 1: _____

Step 2: _____

Step 3: _____

Date Completed: _____

Service & Citizenship

Goal: _____

Step 1: _____

Step 2: _____

Step 3: _____

Date Completed: _____

Physical Fitness

Goal: _____

Step 1: _____

Step 2: _____

Step 3: _____

Date Completed: _____

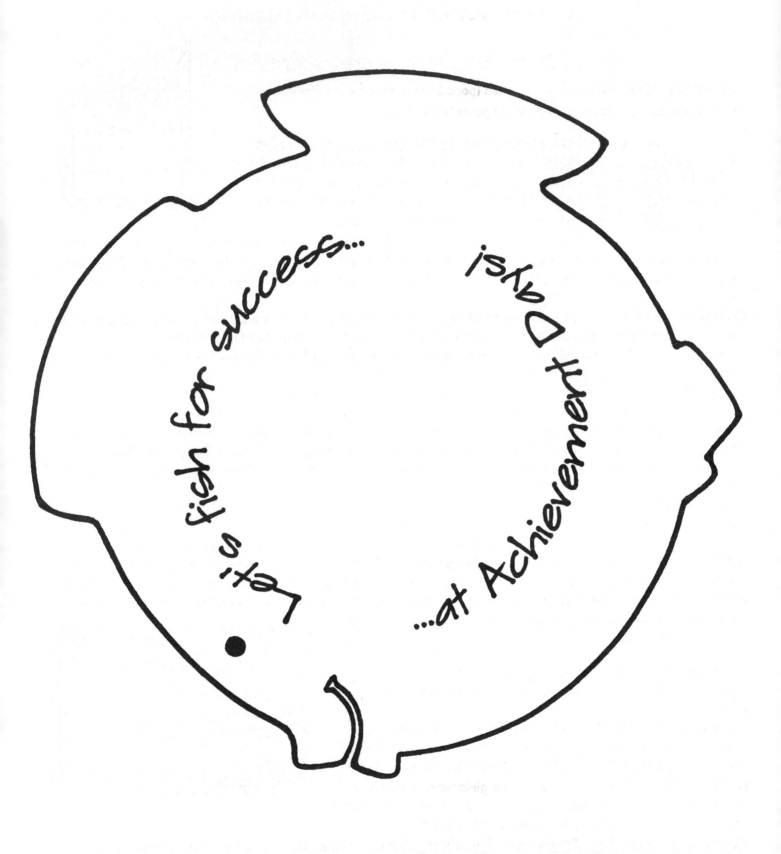

Quarterly Motivation and Award Activities

Theme #2: Clowning Around Carnival

Invitation: Copy-and-create invitation (page 144) to give girls a week before activity. Encourage them to invite their parents to attend.

Goal Motivation Activities – Clown Carnival
OBJECTIVE: Set up five of the following carnival booths indoors and give girls a play money $1 bill to get into each event. Tell girls that this Clown Carnival is their reward for working so hard at achieving their goals.

YOU'LL NEED: Five copies of the $1 Funny Money bills (page 145) for each person attending. Carnival booth supplies (e.g., balloons, darts, dartboard, acrylic paints and paint brush, doughnuts, string, Lifesaver candy prizes, objects for obstacle course, string licorice, 2-liter pop bottles, and Success Snack).

CARNIVAL BOOTHS: As girls arrive, hand out five $1 Funny Money bills to each person attending which they can use to be admitted to each booth. A carnival attendant will take their tickets as they participate.

1. **Balloon Darts.** Set up a balloon dart-throwing booth with a prize offered for each balloon popped with a dart thrown from six to eight feet away. Prize: Clown noses (large gumdrops).

2. **Face Painting.** Using acrylic paints and brushes, have three artists paint girls' faces and hands with stars, flowers, birds, insects, animals, rainbows, hearts, clown noses, fish, or images requested.

3. **Doughnuts on a String.** Hang doughnuts on a string like a clothesline. Have three or four girls at a time choose a doughnut to eat from the string without dropping their doughnut. Prize: balloon, plastic kazoo.

4. **Lifesaver Obstacle Course.** Place objects on the floor two feet apart in different directions. Tell guests, if they clown around and don't stay away from the obstacles, they may lose. If their foot touches more than two items, they lose. Have guests observe course for one minute, then put on blindfold. Turn them around once, point them in the right direction, and send them through. Give a prize if they make it through, allowing them to touch two objects. Prize: Lifesaver candy with note: "You saved your life by taking the right path."

5. **Licorice Lasso Toss.** Give each girl and her parent two licorice strings to tie into circles. Sit pop bottles six feet away from the throwing line. Play as teams of two (girl and parent), throwing the licorice lasso over pop bottle neck to make a ring. Teams take turns, giving each person three tries. Award one point per lasso to determine the winning team, or give those who lasso the bottle neck a piece of Pull-and-Peel licorice or string licorice.

No Clowning Around Award Certificate:
YOU'LL NEED: Copies of the clown certificate (page 144) for each girl.

TO MAKE CERTIFICATE: Color and cut out certificates, add their name, and have their leader sign and date the certificate.

AWARD CERTIFICATE PRESENTATION: Talk to each leader ahead of time to learn specific goals the girls have achieved the past three months. Ask several girls from each class to show or tell about what they have done, then award certificates.

Success Snacks (Ice Cream and Doughnut Clown): Top a glazed doughnut with a large scoop of ice cream. Place a sugar cone on top (at a slant). Decorate hat rim with a tube of whipped cream. Add M&Ms or chocolate chips to make eyes and mouth. Add a maraschino cherry for the nose.

You've just got to come to the

Clowning Around Carnival!

Date: _____

Time: _____

Place: _____

See you there!

Congratulations!

Certificate of Achievement
Awarded to

_____

for not clowning around and
achieving her goals!

Achievement Days Leader _____ Date _____

Quarterly Motivation and Award Activities
<u>Theme #3: Hats Off to You!</u>

<u>**Invitation**</u>: Copy-and-create invitation (page 147), filling in the blanks.
NOTE: Girls are asked on the invitation to "Find a hat that represents the following area of achievement." In the blank, list their assignment, e.g., "Arts and Crafts," or "Hospitality." Assign each girl a different Achievement Days hat to wear (ideas below). If more than 12 girls are invited, duplicate the assignments (for example, two girls can wear an "Arts and Crafts" hat). Give out invitation a week before activity.

Achievement Days Hat Ideas: <u>Arts and Crafts</u> - French beret to represent a painter. <u>Education and Scholarship</u> - graduation hat with a tassel and gown. <u>Family History -</u> pioneer hat. <u>Family Skills</u> - chef's hat. <u>Health and Grooming</u> - curlers in hair. <u>Hospitality</u> - party hat. <u>Outdoor Fun and Skills</u> - cowgirl hat. <u>Personal Preparedness</u> - gardening hat with gloves and flowers on top. <u>Safety and Emergency Preparedness</u> - helmet. <u>Service & Citizenship</u> - nurses cap. <u>Spirituality</u> - halo. <u>Sports and Physical Fitness</u> - baseball cap.

<u>Goal Motivation Activity #1 - Hats Off to You! Show-and-Tell</u>:
Invitation asks girls to wear their hat to the activity. Also be prepared to talk about goals they or someone else has accomplished in that area (that their hat represents). Have each girl model their hat and talk about the goal they represent.

<u>Goal Motivation Activity #2 - Hats On! Relay</u>:
YOU'LL NEED two large boxes with label #1 "HATS ON," and label #2 "HATS OFF," made on two sheets of paper.
TO SET UP: Pile hats that the girls wore in a large empty box labeled "HATS ON." Place this box on the left, 10 feet away from girls. Place a second box on the right labeled "HATS OFF."
TO PLAY: Divide girls into two teams and line up 10 feet away from boxes. At "go," a girl from each team races to put on a hat found in the "HATS ON" box. They race to the front of their team and tell which Achievement Days goal area matches their hat, then rushes back, placing their hat in the "HATS OFF" box. If hats fall off they must start over. The first team to show and name their hats wins. If girls run out of hats, they can draw one from the "HATS OFF" box.

<u>Hats Off to You! Award Certificate</u>:
YOU'LL NEED: Copies of the hat certificate (page 147) for each girl.
TO MAKE CERTIFICATE: Color and cut out certificates, add their name and have their leader sign and date the certificate.
AWARD CERTIFICATE PRESENTATION: Ahead of time talk to each leader to learn specific goals the girls have achieved the past three months. Ask several girls from each class to show or tell about what they have done, then award certificates.

<u>SUCCESS SNACK (Eat Your Hat)</u>: Top a large round sugar cookie with a cupcake (baked in a muffin tin). Freeze cupcakes before placing them on the cookie to remain firm while frosting. Frost cupcake and cookie together and decorate with a frosting ribbon and flowers. Place large decorator candies in flower center. Use popsicle sticks to frost hats. This can be done at the activity.

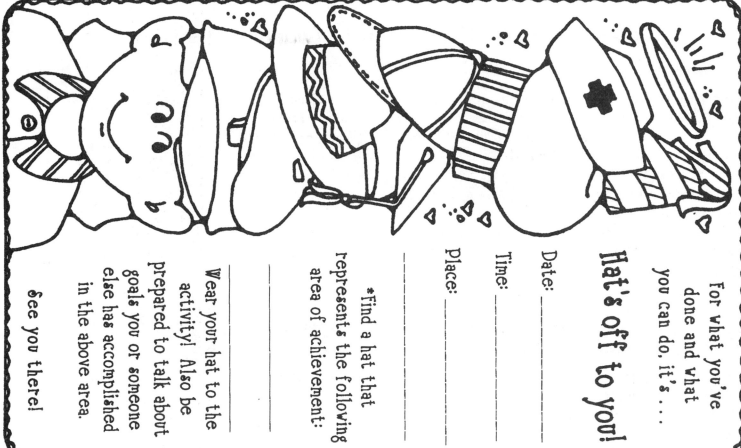

Hat's off to you!

For what you've done and what you can do, it's . . . .

Date: _____

Time: _____

Place: _____

*Find a hat that represents the following area of achievement:

_____

Wear your hat to the activity! Also be prepared to talk about goals you or someone else has accomplished in the above area.

See you there!

Hats off to You!

Certificate of Achievement
Awarded to

_____

for achieving your goals!

_____   _____
Achievement Days Leader   Date

Quarterly Motivation and Award Activities

Theme #4: You're a Star!

<u>Invitation</u>: Copy-and-create star invitation (page 149) to give to girls a week before activity. Encourage them to invite their parents to attend.

<u>Goal Motivation Activity #1 - Star Spotlight:</u>

OBJECTIVE: Have girls guess star spotlighted.
AHEAD OF TIME: (1) Copy-and-create the You're a Star medallion

(page 150) for each girl. Punch a hole at the top and tie it with a ribbon. Attach with tape, curling ribbon along bottom edge if desired (shown above). Place spots of glitter around star allowing a day to dry. (2) Call each parent and ask them to tell you about their daughter's talents; write these at the top of the Spotlight page. (3) Call each girl and ask her to tell you something she likes about the other girls and write it on the bottom of the You're a Star! Spotlight page.

STAR SPOTLIGHT: Tell girls you are going to spotlight several stars. After their Star Spotlight is read, they can try to guess the girl. Have the girl stand and place a You're a Star medallion around her neck and give her the You're a Star! Spotlight page.

<u>Goal Motivation Activity #2 - Stars In or Out Tonight</u>

<u>Relay</u>: OBJECTIVE: Girls try balance stars on a spoon to win.
YOU'LL NEED: A large box of stars, two spoons, and two chairs.
SET UP two chairs across the room in front of each team.
RELAY: Divide girls with their parents into two teams (divided evenly). Give each player at the head of the line a spoon and place ten stars on their spoon. At the word "Go," players rush to carry stars in their spoon to the other side of the room, around the designated chair for each team, and back to the head of the line, turning spoon over to next player to race. If a star falls off the spoon, player must return to the front of the line and start over. The first team to carry complete the relay wins! Award them with stars to glue on their You're a Star medallion (received in Activity #1 above).

<u>You're a Star! Award Certificate:</u>

YOU'LL NEED: Copies of the star certificate (page 149) for each girl.
TO MAKE CERTIFICATE: Color and cut out certificates, add their name and have their leader sign and date the certificate.
AWARD CERTIFICATE PRESENTATION: Talk to each leader ahead of time to learn specific goals the girls have achieved the past three months. Ask several girls from each class to show or tell about what they have done, then award certificates.

<u>Success Snacks (Star Cookies)</u>: Cut out sugar cookie dough into large star shapes using the pattern (page 152) and a knife. Bake and decorate star with yellow frosting and yellow sugar (mix 2 drops of yellow food coloring with ½ cup sugar in a zip-plastic bag. Have other sugar cookies for the parents and leaders, giving the star cookies to the girls.

You're invited to the

✦ You're a STAR! ✦

ACTIVITY!

Date: _____

Time: _____

Place: _____

_____

See You There!

Fold and glue flap to back.

Decorate with glitter if desired.

"you're a STAR!"

SPOTLIGHT of

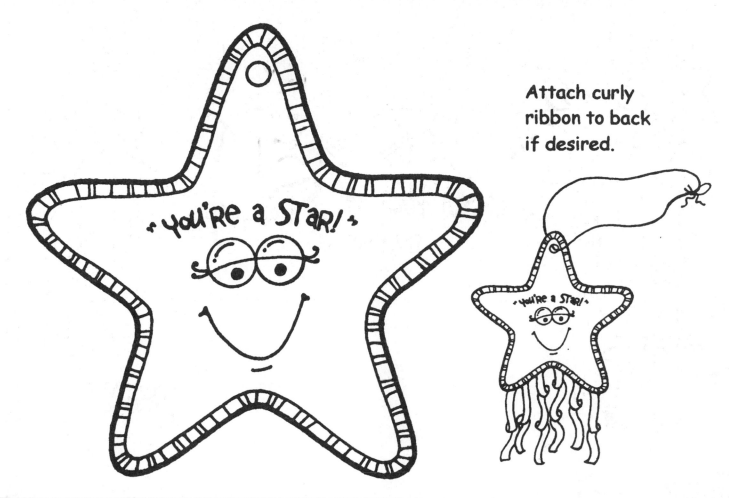

Attach curly
ribbon to back
if desired.

·· You're a STAR! ·

·· You're a STAR! ·

Certificate of Achievement
Awarded To

_____

For Displaying Outstanding Talent
In The area of

_____

_____

_____   _____

Achievement Days Leader   Date

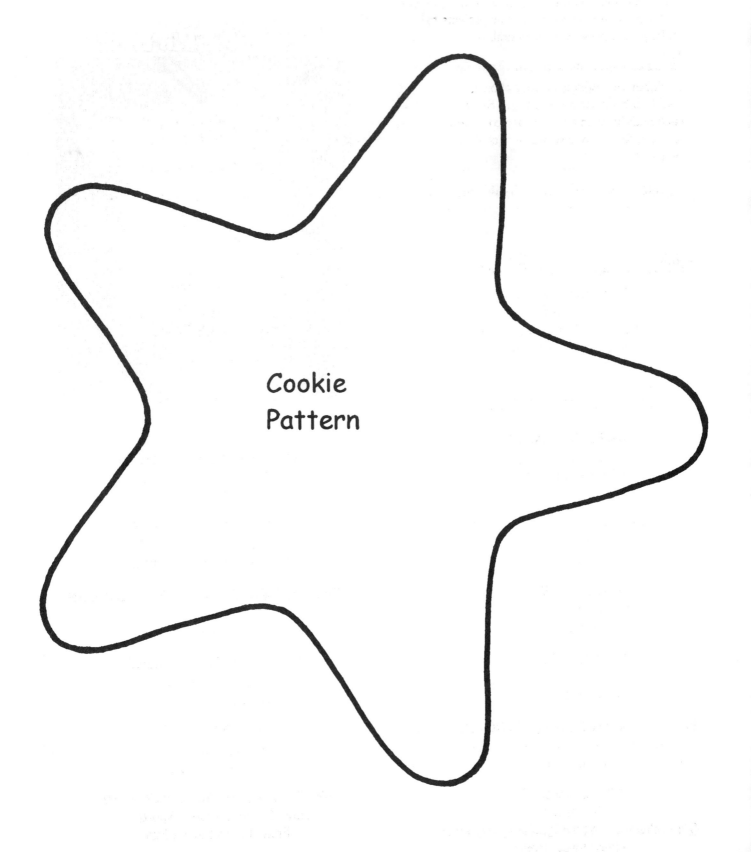

Cookie
Pattern

Here's another fun-filled, information-packed book focusing on each of the Achievement Days goals. Leaders, you will never be at a loss when it comes to choosing activities or projects to make goal achievement memorable.

You can make these activities simple or elaborate. Whatever your choice, you'll all be in for a great time! Start each activity with an invitation to create interest, for a year's worth of "go"al get 'em activities!

Also Available on CD-ROM.

MOTIVATIONAL PARTIES

Pop Into the Future!
Soar to Success!
Dad and Me Western Jamboree
Mom and Miss Pig-nic
Burstin' with Pride!

GOAL ACTIVITIES:

ARTS & CRAFTS
Let's Make Pop-ups!
You're On Stage!

EDUCATION & SCHOLARSHIP
Wishin' in the Wishin' Well
Be a Jelly Bean Reader

FAMILY HISTORY
My Family Tree and Me
Journal Jazz!

FAMILY SKILLS
I Can Cook!
Super Sitter Basics

HEALTH & PERSONAL GROOMING
An Apple-a-Day the Healthy Way
Closet Class!

SPIRITUALITY
B.E.A.R.S.
(Be Enthusiastic About Reading Scriptures)
Home Sweet Home

OUTDOOR FUN & SKILLS
Ladybug Gardening Fun!
Nature Photo-rama!

PERSONAL PREPAREDNESS
I Can Eat an Elephant!
My Cents-able Savings Plan

SAFETY & EMERGENCY PREPAREDNESS
I Can Be Safe
First Aid Station

SERVICE & CITIZENSHIP
Hop to it! Service
That Grand Old Flag!

HOSPITALITY
Friends Forever!
Let's Be Pen Pals!

SPORTS & PHYSICAL FITNESS
Three Cheers for Good Sport!
Freda Frog's Fitness Fun

Mary H. Ross, Author and
Jennette Guymon-King, Illustrator
are the creators of
PRIMARY PARTNERS BOOKS & CD-ROMS
Lesson Match Activities and More:
Nursery and Age 3 (Sunbeams) Vol. 1 + CD-ROM
Nursery and Age 3 (Sunbeams) Vol. 2 + CD-ROM
CTR A and CTR B Ages 4-7 + CD-ROMs
Book of Mormon Ages 8-11 + CD-ROM
Old Testament Ages 8-11
New Testament Ages 8-11 + CD-ROM (color)
Doctrine and Covenants Ages 8-11 + CD-ROM (color)
Achievement Days, Girls Ages 8-11 + CD-ROM
Quick-and-Easy Achievement Days Ages 8-11 + CD-ROM (color)
Primary Partners: Clip-Art on CD-ROM (500 images-color)
Singing Fun! (each year) + CD-ROM (color)
Sharing Time: (each year) + CD-ROM (color)
Sharing Time TEACHING TOOLS (each year) + CD-ROM (color)
FAMILY HOME EVENING BOOKS & CD-ROMS:
File Folder Family Home Evenings + CD-ROM
Home-spun Fun Family Home Evenings 1 + CD-ROM
Home-spun Fun Family Home Evenings 2 + CD-ROM
YOUNG WOMEN BOOKS & CD-ROMS:
Young Women Fun-tastic! Activities Manual 3
Young Women Fun-tastic! Activities Manual 1 + CD-ROM
Young Women Fun-tastic! Activities Manual 2 + CD-ROM (color)

MARY H. ROSS, Author
Mary Ross (shown left) is an energetic mother and has been
a Primary teacher and Achievement Days leader. She loves
to help children and young women have a good time while
they learn. She has studied acting, modeling, and voice.
Her varied interests include writing, creating activities and
children's parties, and cooking. Mary and her husband, Paul,
live with their daughter, Jennifer, in Sandy, Utah.

JENNETTE GUYMON-KING, Illustrator
Jennette Guymon-King (shown right) has studied
graphic arts and illustration at Utah Valley State
College and the University of Utah. She served a
mission in Japan. Jennette enjoys sports, reading,
cooking, art, gardening, and freelance illustrating.
Jennette and her husband, Clayton, live in Riverton,
Utah. They are the proud parents of their
daughter, Kayla Mae, sons Levi and Carson.